HERITAGE—A LINK TO THE PAST  *The opulent spirit of traditional mass design is expressed with a medley of flowers in colors so rich and varied they defy the description "dried." Pink and red roses, blue delphinium, hydrangeas and larkspur, soft green zinnias and bells-of-Ireland, and purple lilacs are processed in fine white sand. Pink and red celosia and pink and yellow statice are air-dried. Flowers, artificial grapes, and glycerinized ivy leaves decorate the gilt Victorian base under the green Italian marble vase. The closed silhouette contributes to the effect of grandeur and elegance and avoids the pompous result that can mar a mass design. Mrs. W. Busanus, Pennsylvania.*
*[R. Stover photo]*

ALSO BY ESTHER VERAMAE HAMÉL

THE ENCYCLOPEDIA OF JUDGING & EXHIBITING

# CREATIVE DESIGNS
## with Dried
## and Contrived Flowers

NEW METHODS OF PROCESSING AND NEW
TRENDS IN ARRANGING FOR HOME AND
FLOWER SHOW

## Esther Veramae Hamél

SIMON AND SCHUSTER · NEW YORK

FIRST PRINTING

SBN 671-20999-x
LIBRARY OF CONGRESS CATALOG CARD NUMBER: 70-159130
DESIGNED BY EVE METZ
MANUFACTURED IN THE UNITED STATES OF AMERICA

# ❦❦❦ ACKNOWLEDGMENTS

It is impossible to express adequately and in detail the thanks due the many who have had a share in this book. Rather than illustrate with the work of only one designer, the author felt that mental stimulation would be increased through the readers' exposure to plants dried and used in many states and countries as pictured by the creative designers of each.

Special appreciation is extended to these generous arrangers who responded so graciously to the request to share their creations. Selecting these few from the hundreds received was excruciatingly difficult. It was like officiating at an advanced national flower show in which all designs pointscored above 95. That dried flower arrangement can be comparable to fresh in design excellence, drama, and creativity is excitingly apparent in these illustrations.

To Lois Wilson of Canada, the catalyst between the author and Helen Van Pelt Wilson, mentor and friend; many thanks to both.

To Robert, whose patience and encouragement have not dried up over the years but continue to decorate our relationship, marital thanks.

# ✿✿✿ CONTENTS

# ✽✽✽ TRIBUTE TO CLEOPATRA

"And I order you to make flowering wreaths for the fete of Janus. And to provide bushels of petals for Caesar's banquet hall. And I demand garlands and masses of bloom to cover my barge." Cleopatra, history's epitome of woman, knew the value of flowers to set the stage. Her fancied off-season demands of about 45 B.C. probably led to the earliest preservation of flowers in the hot desert sands of Egypt. Considering their success with the mummifying process, the garden plants must have been an easily met challenge. Completely preserved groupings of dried flowers, including lilies and lotus, have been unearthed from Egyptian tombs sealed for centuries.

Records show that in fourteenth-century India blossoms were buried in dry sand. Greece and Rome used air-dried grasses and grains with fresh ivy and laurel garlands for holiday decorations. Topiary work and flower, leaf, and cone trees are reflections of Byzantine art. Our ancestors placed air-dried bunches of herbs and grasses on the parlor mantel, dried flowers under bell jars, and pressed-flower pictures on the walls.

Few of us have the snap-of-the-fingers authority of Cleopatra but we have something better—modern processes, techniques, and tools to completely remove moisture while retaining color and form, enabling us to hold flowers in a state of suspended perfection. As a result, the decorative drieds have reached a high degree of social and artistic prominence in recent years.

More people now enjoy flower arranging since they aren't worried about wilting—preservation sets their fears to rest. Formerly many dried bouquets were depressing; they lacked style, dash, expertise, and creativity. This book is an effort to show that "dried" does not mean "dead." Decorative drieds, including seeds, are the essence of life and nature, the backbone of the plant world invisible until the flexible stem hardens, the myriad colors fade, the succulent lushness gives way to a permanent beauty.

No special emphasis is given colorful garden blooms; collecting, handling, and most important, designing with the whole "bloomin'" plant are this book's concern. To show that the beautiful symmetry of a weed seed pod can equal that of fresh flowers, to develop visual sensitivity to the mysterious eloquence inherent in many dried and dormant plant parts, to guide and encourage creative spotlighting of the beauty of the whole plant, thereby gaining for it an appreciative audience—is this book's first purpose. To fulfill this purpose, plant material plays the major pictorial role. Accessories including figurines, baling wire, and scrap objects are subordinate, in keeping with the trend toward what I call New Naturalism where free-formed plants are featured and severe manipulation and painting are "soft-petaled."

It may go against the grain at first, and certainly against Oriental floral tradition, to arrange flowers of one season with those of another. It does seem off-key to combine dogwood with marigolds, but isn't this more a matter of texture and character, of combining robust with refined, rather than plants of different seasons? In this era when greenhouse technology and jet transportation give us forced flowers and exotics at any time of year, many plants know no season.

Going back in history, we find that Flemish and French painters often took several years to paint a masterpiece; they had to wait the seasons through to get the floral models they wanted to combine, regardless of bloom time. And jumping ahead to today (and perhaps tomorrow), abstract and avant-garde designers look upon flora as pure form, pure color, pure texture, and line: not a dahlia but a textured round, not a pussy willow but a line. So if your design, your mood, your challenge to creativity, calls for mixing seasons, do so without apology.

Once you start collecting and drying, your appreciation for plants will be more acute. You'll become visually more literate, more aware of plant family relationships by observing similarities of leaf form and texture, similarities of branch and twig patterns, and calyx and petal likenesses. You'll discover that Queen-Anne's-lace has an old-world charm, fasciated mullein an other-world drama, though both are common roadsiders. Enlist the help of your family. Children are curiously adept at discovering overlooked treasures that have stopped time in its tracks.

It's been argued that flower arrangement cannot qualify as a bona-fide art because it is transient, short-lived. This criticism cannot be leveled at the decorative drieds; many remain unchanged for years. Modern central heating takes rapid toll of freshness, but in this same low-humidity atmosphere, the decorative drieds stand up.

The proud specialty enthusiast can easily, expertly, preserve his Queen-of-Show rose, medal-winning daffodil or iris to stand beside his trophy.

And don't overlook preserving flowers, arranging them, and making contrived forms as garden-therapy projects for shut-ins of all ages. Explore this book with such activities in mind.

Neophiliacs (lovers of the new) have embraced another innovation, that of weaving dried plant parts into the warp and woof of two-dimensional free-form wall hangings and tapestries. A sort of "wallpaper" art, largely concerned with textures and shapes, these are often vividly colorful and reminiscent of both painting and collage, but exploiting a medium uniquely their own. Such "woven arrangements" bring a handmade, one-of-a-kind individuality to austere apartments, offices, and public buildings.

The flowers you grow can reward you twice—once when they bloom and again when used dry, out of season. If your garden is small, preserve a few items weekly; with little care or cost, you will have an abundance by fall, when you can afford to devote extra time to assembling more perfect creations than the hurried here today, gone tomorrow all-fresh combinations of summer. Patience, "the ability to care slowly," and good techniques will give you confidence to custom-tailor your home flower arrangements. Take a cue from interior decorators, from home fashion magazines—no room is pictured without plants, flowers, or fruit. Flower colors and forms enliven dull rooms. But don't let your designs overstay their welcome. Change them frequently to stimulate appreciation. It's your desire for variety that signals removal or refurbishing.

The second purpose of this book is to analyze the creative process, the creative temperament, to suggest how to develop and recognize creativity. Contrary to the general belief, creative potential is widely distributed. But creativity is inhibited by the denial of opportunity for expression. Flower designing gives you this chance to express yourself. The words "design" and "creativity" should not deter you. You use both every day in decorating your home, selecting clothing, in cooking, setting the table. The same need to express yourself, the same innate sense of rightness, unity, and harmony can be brought to bear in flower arrangement.

Loved flowers need not fade; use them to enrich your life, unleash your hidden abilities through designing with creativity.

St. Ignatius, Montana
October, 1971

ESTHER VERAMAE HAMÉL

'Tis to create, and in creating live
A being more intense, that we endow
With form our fancy, gaining as we give
   The life we image.
                                    —BYRON

TEMPO IN SPACE  *Answering the creative summons of the seventies, this design combines the self-sufficiency of a circle with a dynamically balanced seed head and pieces of angelica stems to create inner tensions and spatial excitement. The repetitious rounds are so subtly situated that discoveries involve the entire design. Mrs. H. Cornell, Ohio.*  [*Carpenter Studio*]

# 1 · Creativity—You Were Born with It

Many behavioral scientists, after extensive testing, claim that the imagery essential to art is as universal as memory and that creative capacity is to some degree present in all of us. To simplify, creativity is the ability to bring something new into existence through the reshaping, juxtaposing, and combining of familiar elements. What is unusual, ingenious, unprecedented, but not eccentric or bizarre—that is considered creative.

Emphasis has long been on the development of skills with material gain the goal. But in this decade of the individual, self-development has come to mean inner or spiritual development, the goal self-respect and better understanding of others. To educate toward creativity could be one way to a more compassionate coexistence worldwide.

For our well-being it is essential that we set aside time for self-expression. Most of us spend 90 percent of our time doing things the way others want us to instead of the way we want to. This is robot living. Fulfilled people are those who add a few non-musts to their daily musts. A creative oasis stills the restlessness and avoids the frustration that stems from the disuse and misuse of our aptitudes. As our world grows uglier, we long to find new ways to preserve and create beauty. One way is through our flower arranging. Happily the trend here is to make your own thing within the limits of good design. If it is massed well-grown blooms, well and good. If it is line, a single flower, or piece of contorted bark, and it speaks to you and you are satisfied, that's well and good, also. Both are personal expressions that increase appreciation of floral beauty.

## ❧❧❧ CREATIVE APTITUDES AND ATTITUDES

Beyond one's having a minimum I.Q., creativity is not based on intelligence, and there is no one "artistic" type, age, or sex. Artists, whatever their field, are fat, thin, young, old, moral, immoral, gentle, aggressive, male, female.

There is little difference in the personalities of creative men and women, though men incline to be less intuitive and less able to "see" in their "mind's eye"—both helpful to creativity. In more than seven hundred tests, the Johnson O'Connor Foundation of Boston found that the creative aptitude of women exceeded that of men by 25 percent. Women exercise imagination all day long, while many men are in regimented jobs which limit a creative approach. This probably accounts for the percentage difference. Enticing a sickly baby to eat admittedly is not as world-shaking as the creative areas in which men have excelled, but women's creativity (motivated by duty and devotion) makes the world pleasanter.

Age does not limit creativity. In an Ohio University research project that included studies of the lives of Socrates, Mark Twain, George Bernard Shaw, and Benjamin Franklin, Prof. Harvey C. Lehman, examining 1,000 creative accomplishments, found that the median age for important creativity was seventy-four years.

But if age, brains, sex, and type do not identify the creative temperament, what does? It is the way we respond to everyday experience and our general approach to life that establishes creative attitudes.

Creative people are more intuitive, perceptive, aware. Their attitudes are spontaneous, flexible; they exaggerate to emphasize a point, are more likely to reorganize than to copy. They resent restrictions and rules, shrink from following the beaten path, from repeating a process (even one of their own). Generally, they are disinclined to walk in another's moccasins; they are disenchanted with the status quo, resistant to the "consensus," willing to take a poke at pat answers.

The creative woman is more inquisitive than acquisitive, less interested in floral designs for decoration, more curious about how to relate with plant materials. She finds complexity challenging. In designing, she prefers the dynamic multiple relationships of abstract to the passive, radially constructed mass design. She prefers asymmetric balance to symmetric, dynamic to static, free-form to geometric. She looks with apathy on easy harmony, smooth transition, familiar relationships.

Where yesterday's designer wooed the viewer, new-concept designers plant visual bombs. They have the aptitude of visualizing a complete design, and they work with concentration and enthusiasm to make their vision a reality others can share.

Innovators have the creative courage to break with convention. They give their pioneering instincts permission to explore, shunning the tried and trite. The creative person has the audacity to toy with concepts, play with color, shapes, relationships, juggle elements into implausible positions, to translate from one environment to another, to organize disparate parts into a unified whole different from any design seen before. While respect-

Drama in three acts *The multi-dimensional beauty of free-formed palm bark, which has naturally billowed into a fantastically cupped form, is shown here from three points of view. This stamobile is an example of how inspiration and creative thought can dramatically replace mimicry in developing new forms that incorporate space from any angle. Mrs. G. Psaltis, Arizona. [J. Sheaffer photo]*

ing tradition, they refuse to be bound by it. Their imaginations range beyond the knowable and seeable to the unknown and the not-yet-seen.

## ❦❦❦ APPROACH TO THE CREATIVE PROCESS

How do you approach the process of bringing new forms into being? Explaining the creative process without dimming the mystique is like trying to "put a rainbow in a bottle." No one has yet packaged a fail-safe

COOL JAZZ   *This designer played the "wonder-if" game and was stimulated to put common allium into new perspective, new environment. Expressing the theme, colored plastic boxes suggest the development of the jazz beat, the notes (allium) rising in up-tempo, the colors illustrating the wail of the blues. Mrs. F. Gleason, Ohio, designer and photographer.*

HOLIDAY HUSTLE  *Shock techniques alone cannot create good design, but here good artistic effort has impact that goes beyond formula and craftsmanship. This visual cocktail startles with provocative color so knowingly placed that varied forms unify to give the impression of hurried, last-minute Christmas shopping. Mrs. F. Gleason, Ohio, designer and photographer.*

method of stimulating creativity, but many researchers agree that the process has several distinct stages.

1. FACT FINDING AND PREPARATION OF MATERIALS. Collect available facts. Study ideas of others. Enlarge and add your own ideas. (Facts are the creative interfacing that stiffens the fabric of your ideas.)

2. MANIPULATING THE FACTS THROUGH:

a. *Incubation.* Problem and facts are mulled over while you are engaged in other activities. Ideas ripen.

b. *Illumination.* A flash of intuition, the "Aha!" sensation, the sudden or unexpected insight, usually the aftermath of hours of deliberation and preparation followed by a period of relaxation. Then the under-conscious takes over and previous responses are reshuffled.

3. MAKING UP OF MIND. Fact evaluation, revision, testing, and implementation.

Applying these stages to flower arrangement, you could select a picture of a design, fill the hopper of your mind with all you know about elements and principles, study how the designer applied the principles, list how you think they could have been satisfied another way. Such tactics will increase your design acumen.

Now consider a flower-show problem. Study the schedule class. Ask yourself: What flowers, what containers are available? Review the elements and principles defined in Chapter 9, Collector's Cupboard. Decide on the type of design you need. Mentally adapt, substitute, rearrange, revise, combine, add, subtract. Question combinations, placements. Prospect through books, calendars, clippings. Defer judgment as to workability (even of the obviously ridiculous), until you have made lists of ideas. Select the most promising and feed forward again. Such "brainstorming" may be spread over several days. Creativity is often nothing more than hard, persistent thinking.

Next, drop the whole problem. Incubate your facts and ideas. Take a walk, a nap. Do the ironing, wash windows. Let your mind idle. Stargaze, brood, relax. Imagination begins where facts leave off.

Since you have not simply waited for a bright idea but have gathered much material to fire in your creative kiln, you will increasingly experience what some psychologists call the Eureka-I've-got-it! sensation.

Now to the doing. Construct your design several days before you need it. Examine it often. First thoughts are seldom winners. Make changes as ideas keep coming. You will find lots of ideas waiting to be bent into usable forms. Creativity is sharpened by keeping your "knows" to the grindstone, sparking ideas.

DOUBLE INTERROGATION *The overlapping or the transparency of some elements makes us physically conscious of space and depth. Here the nylon lines, closely strung, obliquely cover one red tulip, leaving the other exposed. Bold directional movement, interest equated overall, freedom from the single emergence point, and open focal areas are new concept handlings. Mrs. J. Wolff, Washington.* [*J. Wolff photo*]

## ❦❦❦ WHAT RELEASES OR CURBS CREATIVITY?

Releasing your creativity brings you the satisfaction of mastering a trend, not just riding it out as a visual passenger. Creative achievement comes when you have so completely mastered the techniques that your mind is released to give personal expression to your designs. Don't be disappointed that each is not a masterpiece compared to the promise of your vision. It is the process of revealing your emotions and the daring to experiment that make it all worthwhile and more important than the results.

To release and develop creativity, you must use it often and with persistence. Try to start with enough enthusiasm to motivate you to completion. We all give up too easily. Self-respect is another motivator, the need to prove ability to yourself. If you dislike yourself, you limit your creative thinking. If you lack confidence in your thoughts and emotions, you may think them not worth expressing. Being ill at ease with yourself puts boundaries around your creativity.

"Overreaching" is still another motivator. Committing yourself to doing something you feel incapable of releases resources, and a desperate effort to save face often ignites a creative spark. Dr. Stanley Krippner of the Maimonides Medical Center in New York maintains that schools stress verbalization and neglect visualization. "The ability to see things in your mind's eye is an important ingredient in the creative process since new ideas often come in the form of pictures rather than in words." You can actually practice visualization in the privacy of your mind.

Highly creative people are dedicated note-takers, even in bed. Alex Osborn, in *Applied Imagination*, calls beds "creative cradles." In a 1967 lecture, Dr. Krippner suggested that we "write down, evaluate, and use dreams in creative problem solving." Rollo May, psychologist and author of *Love and Will*, suggests that we can get fruitful insights from dreams. Dr. Frank Kingdon believes that questioning is intelligence at work creatively. Question the phases of your design. Is a holder necessary here, or more useful there? What if I use this color instead of that? What about a branch or flower inserted there? Pluck ideas from parallels in painting, sculpture, architecture. And always ask, "What *else* can I do to change and improve it?" Play the creative games of "I wonder if" or "this for that"; the "more-so" exaggeration game for dramatic extremes; the "less-so" technique toward simplicity and the understatement that leads to artistic forcefulness.

Expert analysis and constructive criticism can stimulate creative growth. Pitting yourself against another in competitive flower shows can strengthen your creativity. And your self-respect will thrive on recognition. The denial of opportunity for expression frustrates many. Flower shows and flower arranging afford this opportunity.

What curbs creativity? Many people with the technical potential, the educational exposure, the means at hand to create, fail because they lack motive and self-confidence. We must try not to be overly disturbed by criticism, failure, even derision. We must resist the urge to retreat.

Conformity is so dull. Mediocrity is conformity's companion, the opposite of creativity. "It won't work" and "It's never been done before" are slogans of the status quo.

One great aesthetic danger is belief in the infallibility of past methods and the attempt to apply them in a changing era. If we are to have in-

STREAK OF DARK AND LIGHT *A free-wheeling approach to abstract design here results in dynamically balanced placements of strong textures and form-related bleached soya and coral. Placing one soya section outside the container is a departure from the usual that allows greater scope for personal expression. Author's design.* [*Al Ham photo*]

creasing satisfaction in flower arranging, we must play the "better than" game.

## ❦❦❦ GIVING THE DOER HIS DUE

Recognizing and rewarding creativity is a faculty society has so far failed to develop to any great degree. Many of man's greatest achievements were ridiculed when first presented, but Benjamin Franklin, Henry Ford, and the Wright Brothers lived to see the success of their creative accomplishments turn aside the derision.

To appreciate an innovator, we must "refocus" our attention, change thought directions. What may appear to be out-of-focus reasoning may really be ability to see more clearly than we do. Formerly flower arrangers had few alternatives. They were given pieces of plant material, told how high, how wide to make their design, and what color harmonies were "acceptable." While "pretty" and decorative, the results often had a cookie-cutter similarity. Furthermore, they left the arranger with a vague hemmed-in feeling of dissatisfaction, for imagination was hardly permitted and there was no incentive for creativity. As a result, many traditional forms have become visually threadbare, express nothing, and bore the viewer. How much more vital is flower arrangement when designers improvise and explore, moved by individual initiative.

Degree of originality is always an aspect of a discussion on recognition of creativity. Imagination creates an image, but ingenuity and ability are necessary to give an image reality through personal expression. Personal expression is not the same as originality, a term I should like to prune from the arranger's vocabulary. Originality implies one of a kind, something absolutely new. But there is little new under the sun. To state that something is or is not original suggests complete knowledge, and who can claim that? Everything heard, seen, or experienced is buried in the subconscious and may filter through to fill a need even though the arranger is unaware of the source. She distills what is recalled, mixes it with her own creative expression, using what she has on hand, and the result is fresh, and more properly called a personal expression. It cannot be considered a copy or criticized as unoriginal. Indeed, it has been said that anything with 3 percent of one's own expression can be considered original.

We are not all creatively equal. Creativity may occur in modest amounts

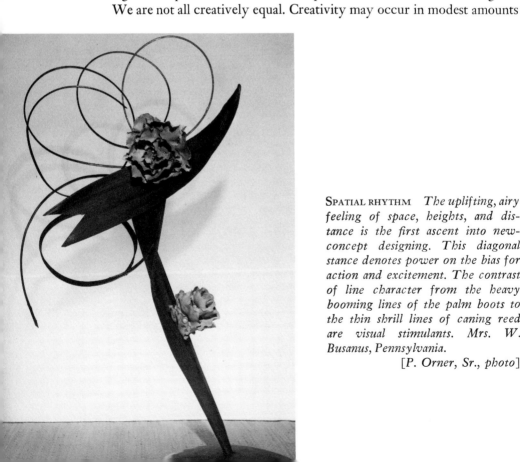

SPATIAL RHYTHM *The uplifting, airy feeling of space, heights, and distance is the first ascent into new-concept designing. This diagonal stance denotes power on the bias for action and excitement. The contrast of line character from the heavy booming lines of the palm boots to the thin shrill lines of caning reed are visual stimulants. Mrs. W. Busanus, Pennsylvania.*

*[P. Orner, Sr., photo]*

but it is no less genuine for all that. It may be subtle as well as bold. A flower arranger who shows sensitivity to color and one who devises a new style are both creative and one should not be labeled as more or less so than the other.

More than three hundred years ago Spinoza wrote in *The Ethics* that "he who begins to love that which he was wont to hate, finds more pleasure in the loving." If you ignore new trends in floral art, you may be denying yourself pleasure. Disagree if you must over the handling of design principles, but find no fault with creative expression.

Creative designers distort and manipulate plant parts to heighten interest, they make familiar forms strange. But the shock of surprise often turns to pleasure when a familiar form is twisted into something new. The "delighting" effect is heightened when common things are presented in less common ways. We have seen hundreds of natural iris leaves. One more natural iris leaf draws no comment, gives no thrill, awakens no image. But when that leaf is clipped or pierces itself or another leaf, thus creating a new form, there is realization that something refreshingly personal has been expressed.

The artistic license to rearrange that which is familiar does not result in design chaos, provided the arranger relies upon the principles of design for control. Freedom to use the creativity we are born with gives free-will flower arranging the life and vitality that bring artistic satisfaction.

# 2 · Decorative Wood—Backbone of Dried Designing

There has been controversy over names given the wood used in floral arrangements. These names may describe a species ("cypress knees"); the location of discovery ("drift" as found on shores, "weathered" as treated by the elements, "ghost" as found in deserts), the surface texture (treated, altered, natural), or condition (dormant, dried). I prefer the general term "decorative wood."

Because nature never duplicates, each piece of decorative wood will be unique, with endless possibilities. Its use automatically gives your design individuality if you allow the strong lines of wood to dictate the design.

Value lies not in rarity, but in the beauty sculptured by nature. The original form can be altered to suit your design by adding other pieces as legs to achieve physical balance, or additions for visual balance or for greater interest. To unite pieces, drill a hole in each, cut a short length of dowel or a piece of sturdy branch of a size to fit snugly in the holes, dip into glue, and force the two sections together using the dowel as a connecting peg.

Some pruning may be necessary to shape a piece for good effect or to remove extensions that obscure the pattern as you visualize it. To blend raw cuts into natural surfaces, rub with gray crayon and white chalk or use the instant-aging method discussed under "Finishes and treatments," on pages 28–33.

Sometimes wood plays a supporting role in a design, but more often it is dramatized as the dominant element. The wood itself may be so formed that it can serve as both container and design element. A cupholder can be inconspicuously fitted into the lines of the dominant wood and covered with matching scraps of bark or wood.

Don't add decorative wood merely as an afterthought or simply lay it over holder or container; rather, employ it as an integral part of the design so well related to the whole that if removed it would be missed.

CONTINUITY PROMISED *As every line direction communicates an emotional impression, the circle here denotes completion and the spiral symbolizes continuity. Dominant round forms are contrasted with vertical and diagonal gourd supports. Since circular shapes attract and hold the eye, the sweep of spiraling decorative wood has the function of keeping the round gourds from demanding too much attention. The pinholder has been made part of the main line by a covering of matching bark, and the design is unified as the eye moves easily from one definite form to the next. Mrs. A. Gantner, Utah.* [D. Blair photo]

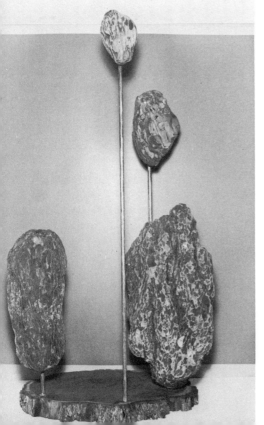

OBSERVATION IS AN ART *Construction, assemblage, sculpture, or progressive design, this is a study in relationships of form and space. Similarity of shapes and dominance of rough textures unify while a unique balance creates visual interplay. The single form, placed out left from the central axis, equals the visual impact of the larger group of forms close to center on the right, and their impact is somewhat lessened by competition with each other. Introduction of any other element would betray the sculptural dignity of this handsome work. Mrs. E. O. Barton, Texas.* [A. Runnels photo]

DRY AND FAST *Here a theme sparks design appreciation. The abstracted jockey (kelp) literally burns up the track (lightning-blasted cottonwood) in this Flower Derby entry which has a humorous vitality between reality and imagery. Space is forcefully used to push under, around, and through the plant forms, exaggerating shapes of both spaces and solids. A container in the usual sense would be superfluous. Abrupt contrasts of rough bark to smooth wood, light to dark, massive to delicate, accelerate the visual tempo and intensify the debonair interpretation. Mrs. O. Blickensderfer, Arizona.*

Pieces of decorative wood are often so beautiful that they can be used alone, mounted like a piece of sculpture.

Designs with decorative wood are ideal for busy homemakers. The addition of foliage one week, a few flowers the next, can change the effect of a single mounted piece.

Because nature does not design in set patterns, many pieces of wood and dried branches do not fit into rigid geometric patterns, like the triangle or the oval, and are referred to as being free-formed. Such free-formed objects are used to make free-style designs in which any additional foliage or flowers are placed to follow the sweeping lines of the branch or root. No liberties may be taken in the twentieth-century traditional way of designing within set geometric patterns, like the Hogarth line (the S curves), but in free-style arrangements the unrestrained basic lines allow for novelty.

### ❧❧❧ FINISHES AND TREATMENTS

Various finishes can be used to make decorative wood blend or contrast with the flora to be used or with the location for the finished design. For instance, a rustic unfinished piece would be out of character with orchids on polished furniture in an elegant living room. But the same piece sanded and finely finished would add interest yet be texturally consistent with the surroundings.

Treatment is limited only by your inventiveness. Variations include:

BLEACHING (may be done at same time as soaking to clean, use household bleach).

SANDING with sandpaper or steel wool.

WAXING (spray-wax for moderate coverage, paste wax rubbed in for heavy application).

SHOE POLISH (clear for waxy sheen, or colored black, white, natural, burgundy, etc.).

SANDBLASTING (usually done commercially).

STAINING (wood stains of birch, cherry, mahogany, etc.).

PASTEL CRAYONS (for shading effects, can be overwaxed).

PAINTING (spray or brush, solid colors, edgings, fluorescent).

OVERPAINTING (effective on grooved, striated wood or pieces with cavities. Spray on a base color, as black, then shadow it by carefully hand-painting the protrusions with gray to bring out a bas-relief texturing for a 3-D effect).

INSTANT AGING (soak in water, rub with dirt and ashes, and bake in slow oven 250 degrees for 6–12 hours).

REVERSE PAINTING (for a unique effect, spray a wood base, container or flat surface with several coats of different colors, as avocado over tur-

CONTRAST CONTROLLED *Intricate formation gives a sense of divided motion strengthened by the various directions of the sharply horizontal mitsumata, thick twining grapevine, and long curve of wood, which was brushed with thin plaster of paris to make it white in contrast to the vine waxed to dark brown. Unity and transition are served by the low cluster of small leafed, dark red Japanese maple. This softens the extravagant gestures of the three branches. Free-formed, free-moving lines and contrasting values give this design a quicksilver quality. Mrs. R. Creighton, Tennessee.*

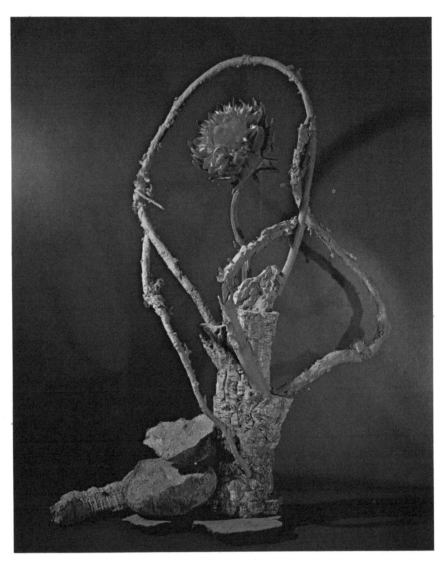

SUNRISE *Overlapping here strengthens depth illusion while creating new shapes and values. The focal area has been de-emphasized and uplifted; the space at lower right equalizes the impact of the high-rising flower. The dominating roughness of the textures contributes a feeling of barely controlled strength and vitality, underwriting our inability to "hold back the sunrise." Mrs. F. Gleason, Ohio, designer and photographer.*

MEXICAN MEMENTOS *The background of this unique plaque is an Indian-bark picture with free-hand inked and painted silhouettes. Wild sunflowers, tiny red morning-glories, marigolds, lupines, sea-holly, and cosmos, collected on a motor trip, are pressed and glued in a random pattern to make a wall hanging that utilizes decorative wood as background. Mrs. E. Bergman, Michigan.*

SPACE WALK RIGHT: *Here decorative wood has the abstracted restraint of a Brancusi sculpture. The two "astronauts," represented by flower forms contrived of seed pods, are symbolically tied to their gently turning "space ship" by bright copper "umbilical cords." In turn the ship is supported by a strong communication line to the dark and square Mother Earth. Materials are wisely restricted and precisely engineered to create a floating impression despite the twenty-pound weight of the featured wood. Marrita Tipton, Utah.*

ACCENT ON FORM LEFT: *In this dignified expression of quiet authority, the vertical strength of the papyrus is barely softened by the width-increasing shapes of peeled and curled wisteria and one fluffy artichoke head. Dominantly different shapes are successfully combined here and variant forms subtly related and placed to accent each other. The wisteria spiral, the oval aspidistra leaf, the rounded artichoke, and the insets in the container design are all forms derived from the sphere, and their use intensifies the underlying harmony. Mrs. C. Bilbo, Oklahoma.* [B. McCormack photo]

quoise over red-violet. Allow to dry thoroughly between coats. Then rub with steel wool to cut down through the various layers unevenly until some of each color shows).

ANTIQUE GLAZES (apply according to commercial instructions and wipe off when the desired color is achieved).

SWISH PAINTING (spray or drip several squirts of oil-base paints into a deep container of water. Dip decorative wood pieces into the water, dry).

PEARLIZED SPRAY (spray to give tired wood a lift).

BARK TEXTURING (leave on or glue on some bark for textural contrast).

CHEMICALLY ALTERED (use oxalic acid as a dip for rosy tones; use laundry bleach for yellow-beige finish).

## 🌿🌿🌿 CONTROLLING DECORATIVE WOOD AND HEAVY STEMS

1. To make the base level, lower the end into a pan of water while you hold it at exactly the angle at which it is to be used; then use the water line as a guide to sawing.

2. Glue a cork to the base to make it easy to push a piece onto a needlepoint.

3. Wrap hardware cloth (approximately ¼- to ½-inch metal screening) around the base of tall or heavy pieces (including candles). Let ½ inch of the metal extend below the end. Secure the metal with tape or wire. If piece is still not steady, undo and *tightly* wrap three or four

nails inside the screening and point them down. (This technique will balance almost anything except your budget.)

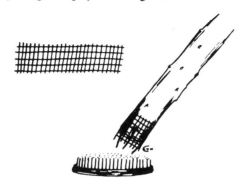

4. Screw or wire a pinholder to the base of a piece of wood and interlock it to the needles of a second holder anchored to the bottom of a container.

5. Mold a large lump of Hard-Set or Model-Light plastic clay around the base of a heavy piece, work into the shape of a rock to make a permanent stony bond.

6. Line a shallow pan with foil, hold your decorative wood or bark at the proper position for your design, pour in thick plaster of paris; let set to form both base and support. After it hardens, remove from pan and foil. Paint plaster to match wood if you wish.

To install a pinholder semipermanently on a wood base, mount it, using floral clay, then drive a few carpet tacks into the edge of the clay so the heads extend above the top of the holder. This will prevent tipping even if the clay lets go of the rough textured surface.

Commercial holders include Manzanita Mount (about 50 cents), which is heavy lead with a screw, and flexible. Swivel-Hold (about $3.00) is very heavy, clamps heavy wood, swivels or tilts at about a 30-degree angle.

# 3 · Dried Foliages for Designs with Flair

Foliages can be arranged alone to create designs with flair and to grace your home without the distraction of vivid hues. In many contemporary designs, flowers are incidental and foliage is often featured.

Only in recent years has foliage been recognized by European and American flower arrangers as having structural importance. Previously, foliage was considered an incidental inclusion in designs composed mainly of flowers, though Orientals long appreciated its strength of character and the ancients copied the forms of fresh foliage to decorate their bodies, their architecture, and their sculpture.

Saga *Dried foliages of ti and aspidistra reveal a vitality of their own as each element in this design flows in a rhythmic visual path based on structural unity, repetition, line direction, and compelling interest. Simplicity is never simple. Here control and discipline bypass the abundance of the fascinating flora available and concentrate on two types, exploiting their many qualities in a design of structural clarity and beauty. Mrs. A. Striker, Virginia.*

Foliages alone can carry an interpretation from establishing the linear
pattern a design makes against a background to supplying interesting
textures, subtle color and framing, or serving as focal or interest area.
(A focal area is always at or near the container rim; an interest area, as
in abstracts, may appear in several places in a design.)

Learn to look at foliage as you do inflorescence (Figure #45, The Collector's Cupboard), for its form, not its name. *Linear* foliages contribute
lift and vitality to line directions with swordlike points that pierce space
when vertical (iris, gladiolus) or, curving, carry the eye back into the
design (Scotch broom). Some types may branch freely and still produce
a linear effect (lycopodium).

The second useful foliage form is *filler*, and this is generally separated
into mass and fine types. Fine filler is used mainly for gentle transition,
providing an easy visual path from one element to the next. Because such
foliage does not have enough character to establish strong pattern, it is not
often used in the newer modern and abstract designs. Rose leaves and
arborvitae branches are examples, and they are often used in traditional
mass and massed-line designs. Broad foliages, such as those of magnolia
and ficus, make good backgrounds for blooms, giving visual weight and
depth. These are classed as mass-filler types.

WINTER DEFIED *The handsome, purple-black Rivers beech, treated with glycerine, provides strong background for two huge silica-gel-dried dahlias in apricot tints with touches of mauve that pick up the warm hue of the pewter-washed copper vase. Easy rhythmic transition unifies, and includes container and foliage forms, the related colors, and the harmonious textures. Timeless beauty with simplicity. Mrs. J. Wilson, Toronto, Canada.* [C. Webster photo]

PEACE PROTECTED *Air-dried strelitzia foliage of strong character sets the pattern in a design with materials that formerly did "not belong together," but the Peace rose is of robust enough character to be texturally compatible with the strongly surfaced container and the dried foliage. On the left, a rose leaf is skillfully placed to complete the rhythmic path left suspended on the tip end of the circle, on the high right. The leaf also serves as a zestful contrast to the circular forms. Put your thumb over it and see how much it contributes to the balance and interest of this powerful expression. D. Moffit, N. Balwyn, Victoria, Australia.*

[Specialized Photographic Co.]

IMAGINE THAT ABOVE: *Forms are juxtaposed purely for their own sake with delightful disregard of identity. Fresh croton and aspidistra foliage (mounted in a concealed pinholder cup) serve as textural and colorful directional lines. The pointed ends allow the eye to slide easily to the bulging rounds of the gourds, which seem to recoil at the leap-frogging cypress root and malformed gourd at their feet. Mrs. F. Gleason, Ohio, designer and photographer.*

CATTAILS OPPOSITE: *Here the painted cattails carry the eye back, making the background a definite part of the design. Placements of the foliage (both painted and dried) contribute to depth. The vivid unrealistic color (DayGlo paint) does not destroy the recollection of a great field of cattails reflecting the blue waters of their habitat and the blue summer sky. Mrs. F. Thornton, California.* [*Monteleone photo*]

JOURNEY'S END *A ship coming to rest with anchor dropped and sails furled is the theme here. The viewer delights in the tiptoe poise of container, the competent balance, the controlled use of clipped green pine and orange pyracantha berries, and especially in the similar shapes of the three elements. Visual literacy comes with practice in searching for form relationships. In this expression obvious compatibilities are avoided, subtle relationships explored, and form finds a startling partner in a container made from a painted turkey breastbone. Mrs. H. O'Connor, Oregon.* [D. Kettler photo]

The third foliage type serves the same purpose as *focal* or target flower forms. Their main value is often in their unique shapes (*Monstera deliciosa, Fatsia, Cecropia*) or their brilliant and interesting color (*Croton,* variegated *Aspidistra*), or unusual texture (mullein rosettes). Mass-filler types like the magnolia can also be used as focal forms.

The "avant-garde" collector will find all three foliage types among common garden plants, by the roadside, and in florist and specialty catalogues. The design you have in mind will influence your selection of each form.

Foliages can be dried successfully by any one of the six methods described in detail under Processes, Chapter 7. These include:

1. Pressing under weights with resulting two-dimensional form. Color often retained.

2. Package drying without weights. This retains some natural contour and most natural color. Used mainly for target types.

3. Liquid absorption and immersion, form retained but color often altered.

4. Air-dried by hanging, standing, or laying flat. Form and color often altered.

5. Granular-processed with retention of both color and form.

6. Skeletonizing. Color, form, and texture are all altered.

Techniques for wiring, shaping, and contriving forms from foliages are also found under these headings.

To GRACE THE HOME  *This arrangement of mainly dried foliages of fine and mass-filler types is in keeping with massed-line tradition. On the left, the far-out single leaf repeats the shape of the space directly above it, and both draw attention up to the high enclosed spaces that subtly repeat the overall form of focal area and container. Leaves in the high center and lower right direct the eye in an easy transitional movement around the design, thus contributing to its pleasing unity. Distinction is achieved through restraint in selection, placement, and repetition. Mrs. A. Meiklejohn, Toronto, Canada.*

[*R. Gordon photo, courtesy* Canadian Collector]

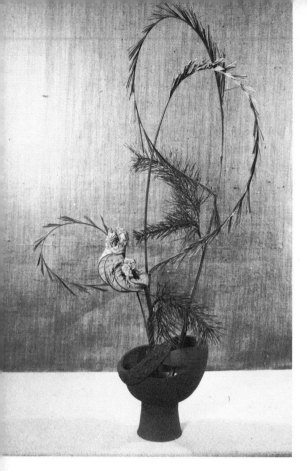

TEXTURAL INTERPLAY LEFT: *Dominance is developed here through emphasis on textures and forms. A rough serrated texture is echoed and re-echoed in Australian pine, clipped bleached palm, and "fisted" cecropia, a target form in an off-center focal area that is balanced by tall looping palms on the right. Form of container is repeated in the cecropia leaf, which was soaked and shaped to develop the resemblance. The structural lines of pine and palm beat an airy repetitious rhythm in which the spaces within play a lighthearted role. Dominating forms and textures are repeated and repeated but so carefully placed that the design avoids monotony and achieves distinction. Mrs. F. Herre, Ohio.*

[*H. Newman photo*]

VAYA CON DIOS RIGHT: *In this collage-assemblage or synectic design ("the fitting together in an aesthetic manner of diverse and apparently irrelevant parts"), the dried aspidistra foliage softens the hard-edge vertical lines and directs the eye to the relics of seventeenth-century Mexico—Christus, sword, and wheel, and up to the lion's-tail plant depicting the worship of the Lion of Judah. Mrs. C. Griggs, Texas.* [*Zetzman photo*]

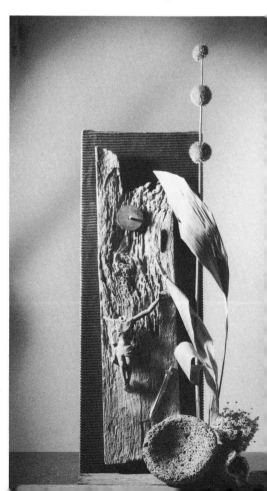

BIRDS NOT OF A FEATHER *It takes imagination to recognize foliage here, but here it is in a design that reverses the obvious and lines up opposites in a whimsical exploration of the possibilities of devil's-claws, milkweed pods, and dried rhododendron leaves and seeds. So used, these assorted materials give, without accessory or need for title, a visual interpretation of a flock of feeding, flying birds. It is surely "outsight" when an artist makes his own insights plainly visible to another. Mrs. N. Reinicker, Pennsylvania.*

[E. Clewell photo]

# 4 · Hang-overs and Hang-ups— Topiaries and Corsages

Limitation of space on floor and table, parties with many people in small rooms, architectural problems, and the natural wish to "do something practical, but different" have brought floral designing to a high level. Plant material takes on a new dimension when elevated above a tabletop.

Aside from the common method of hanging baskets and plaques, the ingenious designer of today uses "hang-overs," such as mobiles and other designs over tables, and "hang-ups," as summer swags and collages for her up-in-the-air creations. Such creativity on high brings walls and ceilings into the area of attention and increases the feeling of hospitality.

## HANG-OVERS—MOBILES

Mobiles are gleeful, merry art forms that are suspended so that their perfectly balanced parts move easily and freely in the slightest air current. Much of the whimsical charm of many mobiles lies in the suspense felt in expecting the moving objects to collide but finding they are so cleverly placed that they miss each other by margins as fine as frog's hair. The motion also delights the eye by repeating and varying colors, textures, forms, and space shapes. The objects chosen must be interesting at every turn as they rotate in ever-shifting patterns.

### ❦❦❦ SELECTION AND TECHNIQUES

The ability to construct mobiles requires a highly developed eye for the beauty of relationships, an exquisite sense of balance, plus strings, fishing swivels, a bucket of persistence, and extra hands of the family. A mobile does more than just hang; it must move with near misses. The actual physical rhythm should be balanced and smooth, never awkward and jerky. Lead shot may be needed to add weight to some objects, thus achieving perfect balance. Fishing swivels set between clear, nylon string and the object assure easy-moving joints. Leaves, pods, bark, decorative

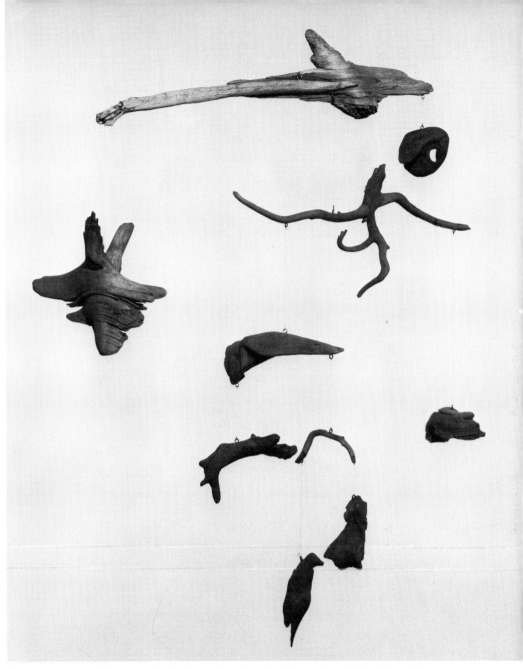

FLOATING FLORA  *In properly built and perfectly balanced mobiles like this, parts are always in motion, continuously presenting new shapes as the ever-moving eye searches for relationships in these small pieces of eroded decorative wood. Imagination suggests resemblance to a hyena, airplane, wormy apple, and bird. The evolving forms are unified by the repeated soft gray, weather-smoothed textures and their similarity of shape. Such mobiles can be time-shortening decorations for business waiting rooms. Mrs. J. Nelson, Nebraska.*
[H. Olson photo]

wood, flowers, and other objects can be part of or make up an entire mobile.

Variations of hang-overs include horizontal wreaths with pomanders, palm spathes filled with Styrofoam and flowers, or Styrofoam balls covered with dried flowers and leaves. A tabletop version is interesting. Cut two 16-inch circles from gray sandblasted wall paneling. Paint the edges black, Mount the circles horizontally on each end of a single 25-inch length of 2-inch dowel. Using swivel hooks and fine nylon cord, hang small pieces of wood, branches, lichens, or burs from the underside of the top circle. Wood bits dip and sway gracefully when glued to flexible wires mounted on a base of bark or driftwood.

## HANG-UPS—COLLAGES, PLAQUES

Many enterprising women have found it possible to combine evening television with the family and the creation of beautiful floral hang-ups for home, gifts, boutiques, and shows.

Plaques and flower pictures of plant materials, glued to a background in a radial pattern, have proved their worth in artistic satisfaction and interior decoration, but today's floral designer has paralleled changes in other arts with a collage (meaning glued or fastened) type of floral decoration. Such collages often combine paper, string, fabrics, and other non-horticultural objects with plant materials. The design ignores radial placement, which means from a single given point (container or cluster

CONTEMPORARY COLLAGE *This artful selection of unrelated objects is fastened to a bas-relief background. The congruous and incongruous elements of contrived cone flowers, drawer handles and pulls, and needle-leaf and broadleaf evergreens are cunningly related through repetition of dominating curves, pinked edges of cones, felt mat edges, and brass pulls. Objects are also unified through placements that indicate a rhythmic path for the eye to follow. Overlapping planes provide back-and-forth dimension to visual animation. Mrs. J. Benson, Maine.*

*[The Picture House]*

WALL DESIGN *Mahogany plywood, rubbed with oil for protection without shine, makes a compatible background for bittersweet from the garden, tulip-tree pods, dock, and split trumpet-vine pods, the seeds removed and the inside painted dull orange to give the vitality of warm color to this predominantly brown-and-tan plaque. The traditional massed-line grouping is balanced on a double fungus base. Mrs. J. Wilson, Toronto, Canada.* [B. King photo]

of stems). The collage may have several emergence points, or no specific one, and the interest is equated over the whole design as in abstract structural designing.

Eye movement, unity, and harmony in a collage are achieved through placement and repetition of forms, colors, textures, and line directions. The eye moves slowly, back-tracking and finding pleasure in searching out relationships and repetitions. In a plaque the eye starts at the emergence point and moves quickly through the focal area and on out to the diminishing boundaries.

## ❦❦❦ BACKGROUNDS

The shape ranges from narrow panels to rectangles, triangles to round plaques that resemble wreaths with centers filled in. Whether the background is polished, natural, gilded, or textured depends upon the overall character of the design. Texture governs choice and establishes the refined or robust character of any art object.

### 🌷🌷🌷 TECHNIQUES

As in landscaping, it's easier to move a plant with an eraser than with a shovel, so it's easier and less nerve-shattering to make a rough sketch of placements before gluing with a strong, clear-drying product. Heavy wood, fungi, and pods may have to be screwed on from either front or back. Large pods and cones should be split in half and used so either exterior or interior shows, as both can be interesting. After the design is completed, a quick misting of plastic spray-varnish or wax will protect and enliven colors. Cleaning is simple; merely pass a clean feather duster or wide dampened paintbrush over the piece weekly.

### 🌷🌷🌷 PICTURES WITH PRESSED FLOWERS

Although pressed flowers lose their three-dimensional quality, they are aesthetically useful in making pictures, place cards, lampshades, divider screens, and stationery. (Use Handi-wrap instead of wax paper for more transparency.) Sketch your proposed design in chalk or pencil on the background. Let your imagination go because this "plant" doesn't have to grow as in nature. Next, carefully select your flowers and place them on the sketch with tweezers, a needle, a small paintbrush, and your steadiest hand.

When you have the whole design laid out, put the glass on for your picture, fit the frame, turn the flowers, frame, and glass over, holding firmly so none slips. Tack the frame in place. A second method is to sketch your design on paper, lay it face up on your work area, put the glass over it, place floral pieces upside down, following the design seen through the glass.

Simplicity and good design are the important goals. Have a definite line to your design, and don't overcrowd it. Reduce bulk by clipping away overlapping stems, but overlay some petals and leaves to achieve depth.

### 🌷🌷🌷 WREATHS, SWAGS, PANELS

Wreaths and swags have become year-round favorites. They eloquently spell a warm welcome that extends from traditional fall and winter to spring and even summer. Made of granular-treated flowers (pages 82–84), such wreaths add a new look to any-month parties. Wreaths, swags, topiaries, and panels are also increasingly favored for decorating churches at holiday seasons.

ORIENTAL TRACERY *This roadside plant is not treated as a "peasant" to be automatically placed in an earthy container, but the rough and refined textures are exploited for the design, their origin unexplored. Wild grasses and Siberian iris foliage, combined with properly scaled decorative wood and fungi, are fastened to cream-tinted pebbleboard. Against this the delicate tan-to-dark-brown flora suggest an Oriental brush painting on fine paper. The sensitive placements, as in nature, strengthen the impression. Delicate tracery and artful simplicity make this ever timely, yet timeless. Mrs. T. Guhman, Arkansas. [T. Guhman photo]*

REVERENCE *A ceramic plaque is mounted on pegboard cut into an oval with a 3-inch border and a brown-painted Styrofoam wreath wired to this. The dried and painted materials are wired to the wreath form and artificial box-wood inserted to soften and complete the composition. Included are jack and piñon pine cones, acorns, hickory nuts, peach pits, pomegranates, and brightly painted smooth and warty gourds. Mr. H. Schroeder, Ohio.*

[*H. Newman photo*]

SQUARE DANCE RIGHT: *A 150-year-old barn board serves as panel background for a collage that suggests a pair of whirling dancers. Dried materials include two ears of Indian corn, artichoke blossoms, love-apples, glycerined magnolia leaves, and red peppers, all visually associated by the rhythmic twists of sisal rope. Mrs. W. Craig, Ohio.* [H. Newman photo]

MISTS OF SUMMER BELOW: *Single sheets of facial tissue are placed on a background, enameled white and well dried, then brushed with a half-and-half mixture of Elmer's Glue and water. Pressed gloriosa daisies, fern, and rose leaves are arranged on the glue, and another layer of tissue added and brushed with more glue. After all is dried, a light swish of olive-green spray further mutes the colors. The result has the restrained simplicity of a good painting. Mrs. L. Freitas, Massachusetts.* [J. Lynch photo]

WREATH WITH A DIFFERENCE *New growth of chamiso, a New Mexican evergreen roadside shrub, gathered just as it was coming into yellow flower, is fastened with greenish yellow yarn wrapped to delineate even spaces. Cornhusks, soaked until pliable, are looped, wired, and attached. A brilliant finishing touch of red chili peppers gives this hanging a distinctive New Mexican flavor. Mrs. C. Viles, New Mexico.*

## ❦❦❦ UNDERSTRUCTURE

Bases for wreaths can be made of coat hangers pulled to a circle and padded with straw, evergreen tips, or moss. Styrofoam circles are commercially available and plywood circles can be carpentered and padded. Since cones and many seed·pods are heavy, the base must be capable of supporting weight without sagging.

Swags are usually rectangular or triangular. They may be simply grouped together in the hand and tied, using no understructure, or made on a Styrofoam base into which various pieces are inserted.

Panels are a more stylized version of the swag. Understructures are exposed and similar to those used in plaques, running the gamut from old planking to highly polished wood, gilded chicken wire, felt, burlap, velvet, even yarn and milkweed floss.

## ❦❦❦ CONSTRUCTION

The construction of wreaths and swags is relatively simple. Drill nuts, cones, fruit pits, and acorns. Then for a stem, dip one end of a Flora-pic or 6-inch length of chenille in glue, push into the hole. Thrust or wire into the framing. String raisins, popcorn, cranberries, and other small objects lei-fashion on medium-strength wire and attach. Don't overlook dried flowers for summer hang-ups. One memorable wreath featured green dried hydrangea blossoms accented with small artificial fruits—a stunning summer-party welcome.

C IS FOR CHRISTMAS, CRESCENT, CANDLE, AND CONE  BELOW, RIGHT: *A versatile and imaginative decoration of cones, burs, acorns, artificial berries, and leaves is fastened to a Styrofoam form. Originally for a stand at a window, this is also appropriate for a buffet table or mantel. For a complete change, the crescent can be removed and superimposed over a full-circle fresh evergreen wreath. After the holidays the wreath is discarded and the crescent stored. To prevent drip on the dried materials, this new candle was soaked in a strong salt solution for a few hours and wiped dry before placement in the holder. Mrs. C. Martin, Georgia.* [*J. West photo*]

HERBAL KITCHEN PANEL  BELOW, LEFT: *An unusual panel-hanging, functional as well as decorative, is composed of two crescents of dried orégano (parsley, sage, basil, etc., could be combined or substituted) joined with a bunch of spicy nutmegs and crossed cinnamon sticks. Pieces can be conveniently pinched off for gourmet cooking. Western Reserve Herb Society, Ohio.*

WEED WIZARDRY *The traditional pyramidal topiary tree, here formed of cockleburs, is varied in outline through the placement of devil's-claws. These martynia seeds, "plants packed for travel," cling to the hardware-cloth frame, just as they clutch the passerby. Only two plant materials are used in this imaginative design that makes visible to all the beauty of common roadside weeds. Mrs. E. Moore, Texas.*

*[M. Herring photo]*

## ❦❦❦ TOPIARY

Topiary work has moved from lawn trees pruned as fanciful foliage sculpture right into the living room and beyond. Interior topiaries are the very thing for gifts, bazaar items, party, wedding, and convention decorations, home accessories, and tray favors.

They range in size from a few inches to an imposing several feet, and in form from round, triangular, cone-shaped, to espalier. Mounted on dowels, in compotes, or flowerpots, they stand proclaiming fine floral handiwork. Traditionally, indoor topiaries are Christmas-tree-shaped and covered with teasel, sweet-gum burs, or small cones, and are used during the winter holiday season. But actually they should not be limited to cone forms, nor their coverings be so prosaic, nor their season limited to winter. The creative designer delights in expanding the original idea.

Variations include:

Exotic fruit cone tree made by gluing shaped pine cones to a Styrofoam base, filling the spaces with artificial fruit and pine needles.

FIGURE 1

Three graduated sizes of Styrofoam balls covered with sprayed cockleburs. Mount on dowel. Or cover the balls with money plant pods, studded with red holly or cranberries.

FIGURE 2

FIGURE 3

Long-stemmed dried marigolds in varying lengths and groups in a Styrofoam-filled vase.

THE VERY THING *Elegant simplicity marks this delightful hanging of gold-sprayed devil's-claw pods framing pine cones that have been highlighted with a misting of gold spray. The Styrofoam base, also gold-sprayed, of this wall or door decoration is accented with bands and a bow of bright green waterproof satin ribbon. Mrs. W. Craig, Ohio.*
[*H. Newman photo*]

Coiled copper tubing covered with artificial and dried materials, or with fresh kitchen herbs (parsley, dill, etc.), and hung with small red peppers.

FIGURE 4

FIGURE 5

Dowel tree mounted in plaster of paris and covered with dried ivy, *Vinca minor*, and gay dried flowers.

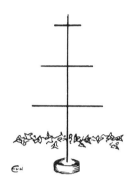

FIGURE 6

Topiary peacocks, animals, etc., formed of crushed chicken wire and covered with cockleburs, boxwood, or evergreen tips. Add a "comb" of bright beads and a necklace of strawflowers.

THE THREE WISE MEN  *A perceptive selection of various floral parts is combined here in an impressionistic study of quiet beauty. Beech burs and seeds, hemlock and spruce cones, fern fronds, cattail leaves, beach grass, lentils, and seaoats are arranged to delineate figures and attached to a backboard spray-painted to suggest the colors of dawn. Imaginative work worthy of the subject and the season. Mrs. H. Bloss, Jr., Massachusetts.*

*[P. Genereux photo]*

NEW IDEA FOR AN OLD STORY *Christmas is enchantingly illustrated here with corn-shuck figures made by the designer. The figures are tinted with oil paint in soft green, beige, brown, and rust, and displayed on a rust-colored burlap background. Gold-paper medallions and gold metallic braid decorate the series of large, green-burlap-covered sardine cans that confine each figure. The three kings carry gifts fashioned from fancy buttons and parts of earrings; the star at the top and design at the bottom are made of beige straw. Mrs. H. Schroeder, Ohio.*

[*H. Newman photo*]

## ❦❦❦ CORSAGES—ART TO WEAR

Nothing quite marks a luncheon, a trip, or a party a special occasion as the receiving and wearing of a corsage. Fresh corsages (received for sweet-sixteen dances, weddings, anniversaries) can be dried intact if immediately and carefully interred in silica gel. No need to take them apart.

Dried flowers are already half-prepared for corsage-making, but the wise maker designs as she dries by shaping and wiring before processing. Tape the stems, group in your left hand, bind with wire. Then position the blooms in a nice design and add a ribbon. Preserved corsages of cones, berries, and evergreens are a common sight, but you will find extra excitement in corsages of dried primroses, roses, azaleas, etc. People will not believe they are not fresh and are amazed to find dried flowers used in this manner. Coat the backs with Tandy's Spray Glaze for durability. Small individual flowers and lightweight corsages can be attached to the bare skin of shoulder, throat, or wrist by spreading on a coat of Instant Garter (H & H products).

# 5 · The Artistic Approach to Artificial Flowers

Contemporary flower arrangement embraces many manufactured products—scrap, machine parts, glass of various shapes and forms, and reproductions of flowers and foliages. Although such "plants" are properly restricted in flower shows dedicated to educating people on the value of fresh flowers in designing, there are situations where man-made horticultural forms are helpful. Artificial grapes, and sometimes other fruits, are presently the exceptions often allowed in standard flower-show schedules. Fruited wreaths and other such holiday decorations are colorful and long-lasting with the addition of tiny purchased or handcrafted fruits made from "Goop." Such products have long been acceptable.

In homes of taste, in clubs, restaurants, hotels, embassies, we are not surprised to find permanent plant materials artistically displayed. At the White House, in the President's oval office and the offices of his important aides, flowers of silk are arranged in colorful bouquets. The adventurous designer may find exotic fresh foliages unavailable or too expensive, so a few artificial leaves strategically placed may be just what her home design requires. Blue is easily found in artificial flowers, but available in fresh only in limited selection and for a limited time of the year. For homes, offices, or meeting rooms needing the accent of blue flowers, the answer can be found in artificial floral forms. However, turquoise is a color rarely produced by nature and should be avoided in manufactured materials if you are attempting a realistic effect.

Plastic flowers come to the aid of a designer when a few more flowers of a certain color or form are needed for a planned design and there is no time to dry more, or it's the wrong season for obtaining more.

In abstract designs where line, form, texture, and color are used unconventionally and purely for their effect with little or no regard to naturalism, a few exotic artificial pieces are often an advantage.

There are two points of view regarding artificial materials in religious settings. Those who feel fresh flowers are symbols of eternal life object to copies of God's gifts. Others consider that well-made artificial materials,

PEACE AROUND THE WORLD *Although crossed lines usually communicate apprehension and fear, here the association of a calla lily, a floral symbol of peace, and the aspiring vertical of dried grapevine have a different connotation. Mrs. L. Freitas, Massachusetts.*
*[House of Photography]*

IN ORBIT *This expressive free-style design communicates the idea with a soaring free-formed branch of natural-dried juniper that thrusts high before it angles to encircle the wasp-nest "moon." Reports of the moon's gray color and cratered surface suggested the wasp nest, the three man-made begonia leaves, the astronauts' description of the beauty of the green earth and man's technology. Subtle lighting heightens the sense of deep space, and the off-center balance, typical of nature, adds a realistic touch. Mrs. R. Reilly, Montana.*
*[DeMier Studio]*

ARTFUL ENDEAVOR *Here the creative arranger questions, then innovates and chooses roots to make a fruit bowl. By means of dowels, two pieces of wood are composed as a free-form design in space, their rhythms strong and intricate. The space and solid at low right, because of distance from center, asymmetrically balance the greater bulk at top left. The texturally exciting wood cradles a restrained grouping of artificial green grapes and apples, whose color complements that of the roots, which are antiqued green-bronze. In this sculptural composition each part flows smoothly into the next. The piece is gratifying from every point of view. Mrs. M. England, California. [C. Barnell photo]*

especially if combined with fresh, are acceptable when handled with restraint and replaced often enough to avoid becoming mere fixtures. Fine plastics, especially foliages, can often fill gaps in supplies of natural plants. The wise course is to consult your church authorities before including artificial flowers and foliages.

A natural appearance is easier to achieve with high-quality man-made flowers in colors and textures that closely resemble their real counterparts. Cheap copies usually look garish and have a thick, unnatural substance and an excessively glossy, waxlike texture. The extra expense for the best will almost always be worthwhile.

There should be nothing sacred about the forms of artificial flowers, which often look stiff, particularly those on heavy stems. Feel free to take them apart; following instructions on wiring techniques, rewire, replacing the plastic leaves with your own dried or liquid-treated foliage.

If lighter wire is attached, the flowers will have the graceful pose of the real thing.

Very large flowers can be taken apart and reassembled with fewer petals. "Welding" can be done with an electric pencil serving as a soldering iron.

Plastic fruits can be "doctored" by rubbing the waxy or fuzzy finish with a mixture of burnt sienna or raw umber and turpentine. Wire these by thrusting a hot carpet needle through from side to side at the stem end or thrust a heavy twig through from the bottom, positioning it against (not through) the upper wall of the fruit. You can reshape and curve artificial stems and flowers by holding them under very hot water until soft. A full-blown flower can be reshaped into bud form by heating, squeezing it in your hand, then dipping it into cold water to reset. Over-large foliage can be trimmed with scissors to suit the scale of your design.

When you work with reproductions, you will fool more people more of the time with the kind of flowers found in your area. Few people

WHERE THE ACTION IS *Parallelism ("placing objects apart on a common base or employing several points of emergence instead of the traditional single one") is used here as an accepted fresh concept of contemporary design. Angled iris lines repeating the verticals of the rectangular containers outline space, as with jigsaw puzzle pieces. The repetition of the strap form of lily petals, wheat forms, and iris leaves, and the overlapping in the lower area visually tie the design together despite the use of three containers and no unifying base. The containers, each with its own holder, support artificial rubrum lilies of texture similar to that of the glycerined wheat, and frost-distorted iris stalks topped with globe thistles. Author's design.*
[*Al Ham photo*]

ERA SPAN *Cherished art objects of conventional type are used in abstract design with a common base under container and accessory to relate them. Here dynamic balance comes into play with parallel placements, objects placed apart being tied together visually. The sweep of air-dried broom carries the eye from figure to flowers. Lines reach out, enabling both placements to share the same space, and they are related through this sharing of lines and base. Resemblance to a recognized object on the left, a sculpture, offers enough interest to offset the dominance of the brilliant anthuriums. Parallelism is controlled by this dynamic tension. Flower placement involves no definite focal area, as is common in newer-concept arranging. Form is repeated with the same sweeping line in thigh, bloom, and broom. Fine textures of figure and flower give this a sophisticated elegance. Author's design.*

*[Swank photo]*

BEAUTY AND THE BEHOLDER *Bones, used here as pure form, are as appropriate as the flowers, the other important form in this controlled design. The upward thrust of the orange-and-blue strelitzias is dynamically balanced by the black-painted bony shape, whose origin is completely concealed. In this stabile, skillful handling of space and form produces a design that defies gravity while suggesting motion. Mrs. R. Lane, Massachusetts.*
[*R. Graber photo*]

expect a profusion of orchids in North Dakota and are not deceived, but daisies combined with local tree branches require a close look to spot the deception. Combining fake with floral is a challenge that adds another facet to your creativity in flower arrangement.

A COLORFUL BURDEN *The beaded, glittering, frosted medley of balls, bows, and flowers in delicate pinks, lavenders, and purples makes an appealing, nostalgic Christmas decoration. All materials are artificial. The airy outline is cleverly developed with daisy-looped sprays, and many contrasts of forms and textures occur in the round mass arrangement built into a pink-sprayed Styrofoam ball. The low nosegay of beribboned purple-frosted roses asymmetrically balances the main design, which looks like a tussy-mussy. Sparkle and transparency give this a gay jewel-like quality. Mrs. J. Rardin, Ohio.*
[*T. Walls photo*]

NEW MOON  The sharp, thrusting forms of the bird-of-paradise flowers, "the shape of the seventies," are softened here by juxtaposition to long calming curves of the protective wisteria. Balance is by the placement; equilibrium would be drastically disturbed if the design were moved to the right on the base. Unifying curvilinear similarities of line and form occur in the three types of plants, but the blunted vine ends, which repeat the squared base, give vitalizing relief from so many curves. Space is used in the twentieth-century traditional manner as part of the periphery rather than being enclosed in the design. Mrs. J. Kestel, Iowa.                                    [*Walden Photos, Inc.*]

# 6 · Contrived What-Is-Its

Contrived plant forms are comparatively new. Fragmenting plants and reassembling parts extends design possibilities for all horticulture. To encourage arrangers to see and create plant forms other than as nature made them does not discredit our medium. Pleasure and satisfaction are derived from fashioning new forms from materials you have collected and preserved. Contriving increases awareness. When familiar objects are placed in a different context, they take on the appearance of newness.

You can be your own hybridizer, your own plant doctor. Contrive "things unlimited" for the joy of creating, to give your designs individuality and distinction, to stop the public in its tracks by the differentness of your contrived elements.

Contrived flower forms (a phrase originated by the author) are not only for the arranger; they also allow the lady who loves the handicraft side of finger work to use flora in her own way, and to exhibit her creations in standard flower shows featuring plant materials. Flowers made of recognizable plants are not to be confused with artificial flowers and foliages. The schedule of a flower show should designate classes in which contrived forms are allowed; and the schedule should also define them as "forms or flowers contrived from unprocessed, recognizable plant materials." Thus, burlap, hemp and rope, wood fiber, noodles, and other such processed plant products would be unacceptable, but recognizable plant materials preserved in any of the various media would be acceptable.

To contrive: Bend, prune or regroup plant parts, and try combinations that cross plant families. The rigid lines of some plants may limit their design use. Examples are cattail and goatsbeard. Removing the heads and reassembling them on contorted stems of another family creates a new design form. This would be well within the realm of recognizable plant material, but one which may more aptly suit your desire to consider plant material as pure form rather than as specific types, like the cattail as it is found in nature.

IMAGINATION BURSTS FROM THE HARD CORE OF INFORMATION *Sensitivity to form and the power of balance lead to the success of this design. Here emphasis on the style and strength of height and graceful alliums mounted on copper tubing and twining to enclose space spell the "with-itness" of today backed by the knowledge of yesterday. By equalizing forces of tension and attraction, this interesting design escapes traditional bonds. Interest areas of dark artificial ti leaves equalize the visual impact of light allium heads; in turn these equalize the strong vertical thrust of the decayed tree core. Mrs. J. Nelson, Nebraska.* [H. Olson photo]

## ✿✿✿ FASHIONED FLOWERS FROM PETALS

Use these examples as a springboard for your own creative contriving.

Make lunaria flowers. Glue the translucent disks of *money plant* to the lower scales of a *small cone*, *teasel*, or *strawflower*, leaving the top as a daisylike center. An easily financed "flower" is the result.

Completely cover balls of Styrofoam with small bright *everlastings*, *strawflowers*, *bells-of Ireland*, etc. Hang on mobiles or stamobiles, or impale on tips of contorted branches.

Wire and tape white, purple, or orangy *onion skins* around the stem and pod of *Clematis davidiana* or *poppy*.

FIGURE 7

Glue dried florets of *primrose*, *azalea*, *dogwood*, or small bunches of *hydrangea* to twiggy branches or *weeping willow* sections.

Use #32 fine wire to spiral-wrap *chenille plant* "tails" to make them stand erect. Group a cluster of wired tails to form a large cactus-zinnia-type form. Or use twisted *bean* or *pea pods*.

Make an exotic form of a dried *tulip* backed by three *hosta* leaves sprayed to match the tulip color.

Take apart at least four to six artificial *lily* blooms and one bud. Reassemble by stringing lei-fashion, beginning with the bud; put the calyx into the trumpet of a partly open flower. Proceed with calyxes into trumpets until you have as tall a form as you need.

FIGURE 8

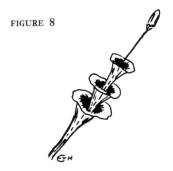

Make shish kebabs of round target flowers, such as *tansy, marigolds, clematis, wild parsley, globe thistle.*

Cut off natural stems. Using an 18-inch length of heavy wire and floral tape, tape up 4 inches from the bottom of the wire. Slide on a flower, tape 3 to 4 more inches, slide on another flower. Proceed to the top of the stem, using smaller flowers and putting them farther apart (or closer if you wish), as you near the top. The process can be used with small *narcissus, delphinium florets, roses,* etc.

Form huge "glamellias" from fresh *gladiolus* petals wired to resemble double camellias. Take one bud, cluster several florets around the bud, and wire before drying in granular mix.

String tiny *starflowers* (after removing natural stems) on fine wire. Cover 5 inches in the center of 5- to 7-inch pieces. Loop, bringing the ends together, cluster five to seven loops around a larger *strawflower* center. Wire and tape stem.

Remove all natural stems from many single, colored *starflowers,* glue directly to *cattails,* which have either been left on their own straight stems or attached to contorted stems of other plants. Cover other seed pods (*milkweed,* etc.) with tiny *starflowers.*

FIGURE 9

FIGURE 10

On the right side of a *palmetto fan*, trim an elongated triangle; on the left side (slightly higher), trim another smaller elongated triangle, leaving three of the topmost leaves full length. Sweep these fronds to the right and down to the left, forming a loop at the top. Hold with a straight pin and glue.

Denude the tip and lower end of *ponderosa pine* by clipping off needles close to the stem, but leaving a tuft of full-length needles in the center of the branch.

FIGURE 11

Glue long *pine needles* or *grass heads* between the "petals" of small *pine cones* or *teasel* (remove the bracts first) to create a globe form.

FIGURE 12

Gather all the long needles of a *ponderosa pine* up to the top of the branch. Bind with wire or rubber band. Dribble glue down into the close-packed needles. Dry by hanging, and respray green for modernistic form.

Cut *canna, hosta,* or *aspidistra* to anthurium shape; use a long seed pod or *petalanthus* stem for stamens. Spray with three coats of high-gloss enamel for natural-looking anthurium flowers.

Poke the stem of fresh *canna* or *aspidistra* through the center of the leaf, forming a loop. Dry. Works with *iris,* etc.

FIGURE 13

Use *magnolia* or *laurel, hosta, lily-of-the-valley* foliage for daisylike flowers. Wire lower ends of five to seven liquid-treated leaves. Group around a center made of a *teasel* or *thistle pod* or *acorn* or small *nut cluster* or *copper pot-cleaning pad.* May be left natural or spray-painted with enamel or flat paint.

FIGURE 14

DUAL INTEREST *Two misshapen sunflower stalks topped with contrived flowers of pampas grass and kumquat leaves are forced between two solid disks of a container that has no conventional opening. The avant-garde position and precarious balance achieved by strong horizontal and diagonal lines give this an ingenious newness. Mrs. F. Thornton, California.*

*[Monteleone photo]*

ALL-OUT MOD *DayGlo-sprayed and mounted on wire coat hangers, bullet-shaped pine cones burst forth, ricocheting in space with downward violence barely controlled by three opposing vertically placed cones. Mod designs employ vivid color and unexpected forms that accent plain walls and hangings, offering dramatic contrast to the severity of contemporary furniture. Mrs. F. Thornton, California.*

*[Monteleone photo]*

STRICTLY OP  *In this nonfunctional capsule table (a flower-show term for an exhibit consisting of cloth or mat, one place setting, and decorative unit, with service pieces placed without regard to function), the intensity of line, form, and color are an exercise in op art. The vivid optic background advances with shrill intensity, refusing to be recessive, as we were taught a well-behaved background should be. A reconstructed sunflower backed by sycamore leaves dominates this high-voltage interpretation. Mrs. W. Folan, New Mexico. [W. Folan photo]*

Make galax roses by rolling one fresh *galax* leaf tightly, wrapping end with fine wire. Wrap leaves progressively more loosely around the first. Secure leaves by stitching with the wire. Galax dries green with no further attention. Liquid-treated leaves may be used instead of fresh. Leaves of *violet, geranium, hosta, spiral eucalyptus, lily-of-the-valley,* and *alba poplar* with silver reverses may be substituted. Use fresh leaves, make the "rose," then dry in granular mix. May be left natural or sprayed flower colors.

FIGURE 15

Make an ethereal "poinsettia" by grouping five to seven bleached and tinted skeletonized *magnolia* leaves around a central cluster of *lunaria* pods.

Cut fresh *paper birch bark* into petal shapes, wire each separately, group to form a large, single, five-petaled flower with green *deer moss* or some *pod* for center.

Combine unlikely plant materials to make exotic forms. Start with a *sweet gum bur* center, add a ring of *magnolia* leaves, and a row of either *wheat heads* or *raffia*. Fantasize some "moon" flowers as illustrated.

FIGURE 16

Wire five to seven liquid-treated *rhododendron* leaves to the base of a bright red *pepper* for an exotic form.

Use loops of split green *cattail* leaves, fresh green *cornhusks, Scotch broom,* or *aspidistra* about ¼ to ½ inch wide. Wind each strip around three fingers, three or more times. Twist wire around base of loops, extending wire down for stem. Tape. Group or use singly.

Or make a 1-inch loop, tape to heavy wire, alternate down the wire, adding more loops of increasing size in same way as reassembling a spike-type flower. Spray flower colors.

Or snip off point of a cone paper cup. Wrap strips of *reed* or *raffia,* etc., over the edges, threading through the bottom. Wire and tape at the base for tulip form.

Surround large green pepper petals (dried and wired) with rubber-plant leaves wired upside down.

FIGURE 17

## ❦❦❦ CORNHUSK VERSATILITY

Separate husks, dry two weeks or more. Then place in hot water five minutes; wrap in damp newspaper to keep pliable while you work. If you want a smooth texture, press the leaves with a warm iron. May be left natural beige, tinted, or bleached. Centers or edges may be brushed with water colors. Wire each husk leaf and assemble around *everlastings* or *grass heads* as centers. We commonly see simple rose forms, but try lilies, orchids, daffodils, dogwood, carnations, and fantasied forms. Use in any type design, wreath, topiary, mobile, corsage.

DAISY. Cut twelve large 5-inch daisy-shaped petals from *husk* or *aspidistra*. Spray with one-coat enamel. Make a crease down the inside center by folding lengthwise. Spray with another coat or two of enamel. Add wire. Assemble around a bright yellow *plastic pot cleaner.* Tape.

FORGET-ME-NOTS. Knot centers of 3½-to-4-inch by ¼-to-½-inch-wide strips of *husk, straw* or *reeds* or fine foliage like *cornlily.* Bring ends of knotted strips together, bind, tape.

SWEET PEAS. Cut two rose-petal-shaped pieces of dyed *cornhusk.* Place one slightly lower than the other, bind with medium wire, tape. Shape the lowest petal to resemble sweet peas.

FANTASY FORM. Cut five 5-inch strap petals similar to iris falls. Arrange around a bright, dried red *pepper,* wire, and tape to auxiliary stem. Reflex the *cornhusk* petals down around stem, leaving the pepper standing free for an exotic form similar to shampoo ginger flowers.

ACCENT ON LINE AND SPACE *The sinuous, plastic interplay of fasciated mullein and sunflower trumpets creates repetitive space forms. Contrast of light and dark values prevents monotony and establishes depth as the dramatically shaped elements interweave, first in front, then in back of the dominant main line. Mrs. J. Jarboe, Washington.*

FIGURE 18

### ❧❧❧ FORMS FROM PODS, NUTS, CONES, SEEDS, LICHENS

Split *Chinese lantern pods* before they dry so they will curl into rosettes of unusual shape.

Cluster male *pine tree pollen pods*. Wire many pieces of *palm* ribbon around the cluster, using a thorny *rose* branch upside down for stem.

FIGURE 19

Dip the stem ends of *bean pods, pine needles,* or *grass* in glue and insert into *cones, teasel,* or *thistle pods.* Using the same suggested centers you may substitute *corn kernels, pecan husks, pumpkin seeds,* or *pine cone* "petals" in single or double rows to make very real-appearing flowers. Leave natural or spray.

Re-form *goatsbeard* (wild salsify) into various ethereal shapes. First, spray with a slow-drying gloss enamel or varnish; then, before this dries, hold the ball upside down and release the puff from its base. Pull gently to flatten and shape into large stars, triangles, circles, etc.

Glue *water hemlock* into centers of *thistle pods,* which are still on the natural stems. Especially effective if thistle has been contorted by roadside sprays.

Glue *trumpet bean pods* around a large *sunflower.*

Soak dissected, beaded strings of dried *palm* or *philodendron* aerial roots in warm water to curve or to balloon. To balloon, tie ends tightly and set base in a holder.

Spread pods and foliage of any type (*tulip, peony, wood roses, milkweed pod* interiors, or heavy leaves like *croton*) with glue; before they dry, sprinkle with crushed eggshells, rice, seeds, black or white sand, crushed Christmas tree ornaments, or glass chips.

Make *milkweed* or *tulip tree* "poinsettias." Select five red-painted sections, wire each. Assemble in a flat single pattern around a cluster of green *deer moss, eucalyptus,* or artificial *berries.* Tape stems into a single one. Make some larger, some smaller. The center cluster can be encircled with another row of *everlastings* or *feverfew* before assembling.

FIGURE 20

Make *milkweed* or *yucca* "tulips" by rounding off pointed tips of four pods. Spray-paint desired color. Wire and Floratape or cluster the pods around a large fluffy dried *carnation* or *marigold.* Arrange so the flower is pushing out of the pod cup, or fill the pod cup with *deer moss.*

FIGURE 21

Wire many individual *yucca* or *milkweed pods* and group in the form of a huge football chrysanthemum.

Brush all seeds from the flattened areas of fasciated *mullein,* leaving rough seeds on the edges. Or brush seeds off all raised surfaces, leaving depressed areas nubby with seeds. A third way is to strip off seeds to the tip, leaving only the ends textured.

Glue distorted *mullein* heads to tops of Swiss-cheesy *cholla cactus* skeletons to achieve texturally unique form and line material. Or attach to ends of contorted branches of *corkscrew willow*.

Dowel-mount dried *corncobs* (after kernels are removed) for unusual textured forms. Leave natural or spray color on.

To make popcorn chrysanthemums, stick popped corn kernels to one another with clear craft glue; or glue popped corn to Styrofoam balls of varying sizes. Insert plastic stems or glue to natural stems after spraying balls bright yellow.

For popcorn cattails, thread 12 to 25 popped kernels, one at a time, to top of heavy wire or plastic stem. Spray brown.

Impale a *peanut* still in shell on wire, dip in shellac. Wire a cluster into a blossom form or use lei-fashion for line accents, or shape into a grape cluster. Spray if desired.

Spread out a *copper pot scourer* and enmesh *bur-oak acorns, pecans, filberts,* or *peanuts* into grapelike clusters. Or cover each with plastic wrap (dip in boiling water to shrink) or use a 4- to 5-inch square of nylon hosiery. Wire, tape, adding a few liquid-treated leaves of proper size. Add a few tendrils by spiraling a 9-inch piece of taped wire around a pencil. If you prefer a more natural-looking cluster, drill a hole in each nut or *larch cone* and wire into grapelike clusters. Vary by melting candles and dipping pecans after drilling but before wiring into clusters of thirty nuts per bunch. Dip approximately twelve times to get a soft color.

Slice wheels from large *cones* or rainbow *corncobs* (with kernels attached). Use chartreuse *deer moss, eucalyptus,* or *goldenrain-tree pods* for centers. Hook-wire (pages 100–1) to add stems.

Split large *pine cones* from tip to base for unusual tree forms; mount on stems if desired.

Bake *Aleppo pine cones* in slow oven until the tightly closed scales open. Drill holes 1 inch deep in cones. Glue onto auxiliary stems or slice and wire with a cluster of green *eucalyptus* as center.

Glue "petals" from large *pine cones* to centers made of *cornstalk,* sliced into rounds.

FIGURE 22

Spray *sweet-gum balls* or *teasel* desired color or silver. Wire and tape. Glue on sprayed glittered toothpicks to give porcupine effect.

FIGURE 23

Strip all the top "petals" from a *deodora pine cone,* leaving only a bottom row or two; leave the center core as a unique enlarged "stamen."

FIGURE 24

String *cranberries, juniper, bayberries* lei-fashion on medium-fine wire. Loop, bind five to seven loops with medium wire and Floratape ends into one main stem. Dip into alcohol-shellac. May be spray-painted.

Select a dried, moldy *lemon* for an interesting design form.

Wire bunches of dried *broccoli*. Cluster and tape for unique green, highly textured floral forms, or use smaller pieces in corsages or for centers of other contrived forms.

Refract *wheat* or *grass stems* 1 inch from base of head. Spiral-wrap stems with medium-fine wire. Tape. Heads will form a ray-petaled composite "flower." Use as many heads as needed for the size flower you want.

Glue *pampas grass* into stuccolike spires with wallpaper paste (or use instant papier-mâché mix, gesso, or spackle). Spray-paint psychedelic colors for strong, textural, linear material.

### ❧❧❧ VEGETABLES, FRUITS, AND BERRIES

Slice ¾-inch wheels of *Osage orange*. Air- or oven-dry. See Collector's Cupboard, Chapter 9.

### ❧❧❧ BRANCHES

Drill holes in ends of *strawberry popcorn*, fill with glue, and thrust onto pointed ends of interestingly shaped branches, or thrust red *peppers* on the branch ends.

Peel green *honeysuckle* or *wisteria* branches and wrap around a container. Wire secure until dried. Remove wire and add other forms to complete a design. Fresh *okra* and *locust pods* can be shaped this way.

FIGURE 25

Glue *okra, sunflower, milkweed, devil's-claw*, plastic *pine tips*, dried *mushrooms, cattail* tops, *goatsbeard*, etc., to ends of contorted branches.

### ❦❦❦ FRUIT PEEL

Make peel flowers. Using largest pieces of citrus peel, cut wheel spokes, leaving a central hub un-clipped. Wire by hook method. Fit into an old cup during oven-drying to set shape (100 degrees 4 to 5 hours). May be sprayed. Strip off *timothy grass seeds*, leaving only a tuft at the end of the head. Assemble with "stamen" tufts rising high above peel petals.

ALL OURS TO USE CREATIVELY *Frankly fake sunflowers have centers made of crushed brown glass embedded in plastic with gold drapery hooks glued to the outer edges, after being filled with liquid yellow plastic. The cattails, pieces of plastic tubing sprayed brown, are coated with glue and also rolled in finely crushed glass. Smaller flowers and spike material at top and side give easy visual movement from the large focal flower. Liquid-treated foliage completes a casual but effective design. Mrs. H. Hunter, Ohio.*

FIGURE 26

Lay *banana* peels on cement in the hot sun after pushing a wire into the stem end. Place three dried peels, one on top of the next; glue a pod or flower in the center to get an exotic black form similar to an orchid-flowering dahlia.

### ❧❧❧ FRANKLY FAKE AND FUN FLOWERS

Find *saguaro* boot "flowers." A search of fallen cacti will turn up boots, which resemble huge tulips, broad single roses and fantastic moon forms. No further treatment is needed on these hard scar-tissue nests pecked by desert birds. Wash, drill holes in the bottom, and mount on heavy wire or sticks. Glue *deer moss* or *everlastings* in centers. May be left natural gray with orangy blendings or spray-painted a floral color.

Cover three straight sticks of varying heights (*bamboo, cattail, cornstalks*) completely with glued-on *moss* or small *everlastings*.

Spray small *kitchen bottle brushes* orange-red; they will resemble flowers of the warm-climate shrub called bottle-brush.

Slice *bamboo* diagonally and mount on a pinholder; paint the inside.

Place (leaving spaces between) large colored or natural wooden *beads* on *swamp grass, broom,* or *cattail* stems.

Cut a flower, leaf, or fantasy form from empty *honeycombs*. Mount on stems. Use in their natural state or spray-paint.

Buy *noodles* and *macaroni* in a variety of wonderful forms—bows, coils, wheels, shells, fluted ribbons, etc. Using wire and tape, and imagination, make large round flowers of fluted ribbons, or string wheels and flutes lei-fashion for spike forms, or group several straight spaghetti spears to simulate Scotch broom.

Make a straw leaf by taking a long piece of chenille wire stemming and, beginning at the tip, knot on a 12-inch length of damp straw (using the first one-half tie of a granny knot). Proceed down the stem for 5 to 8 inches, taping straws on at ½-inch intervals. Using scissors, cut straws off to a point at the tip, but leave full width at the bottom for an interesting leaf form.

Try safety-pin flowers. Select a small Styrofoam ball or *sweet-gum ball* or *teasel* pod. Spray silver. Straighten large *safety pins* so you have a point on one end, hook on the other. Jab the pointed end of each pin into the ball, covering it with the pins. Mount balls on stems. May be sprayed vivid colors if the natural silver color does not fit your design needs. Stand pins in a block of scrap Styrofoam during painting if you want them a different color from the ball.

Make a hairpin flower. Select three sizes of blond *hairpins*. Insert them in circles around a small black-painted *Styrofoam* or *sweet-gum ball* or *teasel* pod. Mount on stem. If hairpins of other than a natural color are needed, support in Styrofoam and spray.

Use small *marshmallows* for stamens and flower centers. If smaller size or shape is needed, roll and re-shape. Marshmallows may be spray-painted wild colors and glittered. Miniature marshmallows may be strung lei-fashion and looped to form petals of a larger flower.

Make apple-doll faces for corn-husk figures. Peel a hard, firm *apple*. Split in two. Spray sections with a solution of benzoate of soda as a preservative. Age the pieces on a window sill in dry air with plenty of ventilation. Leave 3 to 4 weeks. When apple becomes like soft putty, pinch out features of chin, nose, lips, eye sockets. Insert bead-headed pins for eyes. Set aside to dry until hard and a deep copper color. Characteristic wrinkles develop as the apple shrivels and need not be pressed in. Mount on a wire structure. Add *cornhusk* or *fabric clothing* indicative of pioneers, Indians, etc. Faces may also be carved when apple is fresh, and then shellacked. Use as accessory or sales item.

### ❦❦❦ CRAFT GOOP

This is an easily, inexpensively made art dough valuable for the making of tiny fruits, vegetables, foliage, and flowers for use on topiary trees, della Robbia wreaths, etc.

*Goop Recipe #1.* Mix 1 cup cornstarch with 2 cups salt. Add and stir in 1½ cups water. Cook, stirring constantly until all the water is cooked out, and the mixture becomes too stiff to stir. Knead like dough, dusting hands with cornstarch, and work surface with additional cornstarch. Shape. Dry for 1 week. Wrap unused dough in foil or plastic bag to store. Keeps 30 days.

*Goop Recipe #2.* Mix 2 cups salt with ⅔ cup water. Stir over heat 3 to 4 minutes. Remove and add 1 cup cornstarch which has been dissolved in ½ cup cold water. Stir quickly. Mix well; will be like stiff dough. Shape, dry 1 week.

*Goop Recipe #3.* (Recommended for patio and tree decorations and figures on wire or mesh armatures.) Mix 4 cups flour, 1 cup salt, and 1½ cups hot water. Knead dough until pliable. Tint small batches with vegetable coloring. Or coloring may be added to the hot water for large batches of one color and for best results. Form into desired shapes. Bake in 250-degree F. oven approximately 4 hours. When Goop cools, paint as desired. Spray with clear lacquer to preserve.

*Hints for fruit forms:* Use cloves or twigs for stems. To give a natural-looking texture, roll strawberries in mustard seed, avocados in grits, oranges on a needle frog. Color with melted crayons. Paint or apply shoe polish.

*Note to flower show exhibitors:* Check the schedule rules closely to ascertain if fantasied forms contrived from combinations of organic (plant materials or once-living items) and inorganic items (safety pins, hairpins, artificial stamens, etc.) are acceptable.

# 7 · Processes of Preservation

Modern techniques have brought changes in the various processes for preserving plant materials. Among these are liquid solutions, granular mixtures (other than sand, borax, and cornmeal), and freeze-drying. Antifreeze is an acceptable substitute for the more expensive glycerin and can be used as successfully in many cases. Pumice, laundry detergents (Bold), and perlite (crushed volcanic rock obtained from building-supply companies) are all fairly fast-acting and inexpensive, as is Kitty Litter. Enzyme-active presoak laundry granules (Axion) are effective, being lighter and quicker than sand mixtures and having the advantage over meal-mix of depositing less powder that must be brushed off delicate dried petals. Color is well retained, but not so successfully as in silica gel, which remains the "Cadillac" of granular treatments.

Freeze-drying is an exciting breakthrough, but the process is incompletely tested at this point. It is reported that actual flowers are preserved by quickly drawing out the moisture through a fast-freezing process. Elaborate equipment is needed and not normally available to flower hobbyists. Florists and department stores will probably handle these flowers that reportedly last six to twenty-four months, depending on the dryness of the atmosphere.

## ❦❦❦ DRYING TIME NEEDED

It takes a nice sense of nick-of-timing to keep your various media going all summer. By using all the processes, you can space and plan so both granular and liquid media are working even while you vacation. The time needed depends on the moisture content of the plant as well as the humidity in your area and the process used. See Chapter 9, Collector's Cupboard, and each process for specifics, but generally:

Silica gel requires 48 to 72 hours;

Other granular mixes require 3 to 4 days to 2 to 3 weeks;

Liquid treatment takes 3 days to 3 weeks;

Skeletonizing, waxing, varnishing, crystal-dipping require several hours each.

Once you've tried drying flowers, you'll realize how simple, yet challenging, the process is, and it will be June in January when your garden is well preserved.

# CAPRICES OF COLOR

The preservation processes cause many flower colors to act in a fickle, whimsical, even freakish manner. A vivid color after drying (or a faded or speckled hue) may be natural for the variety, so don't blame your medium without full testing. Granular-dried colors tend to intensify. Pink becomes red, and many red flowers contain some blue (when fresh red flowers begin to fade, we say they are "bluing"), making it difficult to get a pure preserved red. Best results are achieved by selecting deep pinks ('Charlotte Armstrong' roses) and by choosing reds that tend toward orange, not blue. A simple test of color is to peer through almost closed lashes; this screens out surrounding hues.

REDS dried in silica gel or Axion hold better because of the shortened drying time. Salt added to the usual borax-meal-sand mixes has a color-stabilizing effect. The reds of celosia, of orange-red and deep pink roses, strawflowers, *Salvia splendens*, and some berries (holly, polygonum, nandina, pyracantha) are less fugitive than most.

PURE BLUE is difficult to find even in fresh flowers, and when dried tends to turn toward lavender or purple. Larkspur, hydrangea, salvia, anemone, delphinium, and clematis are best choices.

YELLOW flower pigments are usually unaltered or may even become intensified after drying. Evening primrose is an example. Yellows in roses, zinnias, daffodils, yarrow, marigolds, goldenrod, rudbeckia, gloriosa daisies, strawflowers, and pansies successfully hold their hues.

VIOLETS AND PURPLES tend to darken disappointingly. The rather harsh magenta of the perennial sweet pea, however, becomes a much lovelier and more usable soft lavender, while pink zinnias with blue in their make-up approach magenta when dry.

WHITE is much needed; it is a good modifier and in a mass design is needed for transition and the blending of incompatible hues. For instance, the purple-red of buddleia and veronica can be used close to orange-red roses if a bit of white larkspur or Queen-Anne's-lace is placed between them. White flowers are whiter if speed-dried with additional heat, or if done in Axion or silica gel. Fresh magnolia and rubber-plant foliages boiled in very soapy water will turn white.

GREEN is fickle and shifts widely, due to chlorophyll displacement. Hydrangea, globe-thistle buds, and ferns are good choices for natural greens. Liquid treatment by stem absorption of glycerin or antifreeze may remove most or all the green, depending upon the length of time the materials are left in the solution. Completely glycerined foliages are, in most cases, a mellow brown. The greens of pressed or hang-dried foliages usually soften to grayed green. Hosta, violet, and lily-of-the-valley stay bright green when speed-dried or antifreeze-immersion treated. The vivid yellow-green of iris foliage becomes green-brown after glycerinizing. Lilac and rose foliages stay a fairly normal green after granular drying.

# GRANULAR PROCESSES

Even beginners will have immediately satisfying results with granular drying. Try all the flowers in your garden. You'll be delighted with some, disappointed by others, and surprised by the lifelike permanence of many. Keep simple records to avoid wasting time and materials next year on unsatisfactory flowers. One advantage of the granular media over the old-fashioned hanging or pressing methods is that both form and color of flowers are preserved and shrinkage is considerably reduced. Sift the medium occasionally to remove broken petals and reuse year after year.

### ❦❦❦ SILICA GEL

Purchase ready-mixed under trade names of Flower-Dri, Flora-Cure, etc. The coarse brown type is generally unsatisfactory. Silica gel is the most successful and fastest granular process. Results are excellent, but the medium is more expensive than others ($1.50 to $2.00 per pound). Drying time is considerably shortened (minimum two days), which gives opportunity to dry a number of batches before blooming season ends. Five pounds is sufficient for the average hobbyist, who will want to use silica gel for her most choice blooms as the shortened drying time also results in brighter, truer, more typically natural colors.

Silica gel contains blue crystals that turn pinkish when moisture-laden; they are used as moisture meters to tell you when the medium needs drying out (usually after every two to three uses). Do this by spreading out in a large flat pan and placing in a 250-degree F. oven for approximately 30 minutes. When the crystals are blue again, they are ready for reuse. It is imperative for good results that you watch the blue indicator crystals closely: silica gel is unique in that it may be soaking wet and still feel and appear bone-dry to touch and eye. It is harmless, so don't be afraid to handle with your bare hands. Keep silica gel in an airtight container at all times, particularly when using to dry specimens.

### ❦❦❦ ENZYME-ACTIVE LAUNDRY GRANULES (AXION)

Use as poured from the package or mix half and half with cornmeal or Bold detergent. Results are relatively fast (three to four days) and colors hold well. The fluffy texture will not crush delicate petals and little dust is left to brush away. The container may be left uncovered during processing.

### ❦❦❦ DETERGENTS

May be used as poured from the package or mixed, 2 cups with 4 cups cornmeal. This makes a fluffy, non-deteriorating mix that dries flowers in four to seven days. One cup borax may be added.

### ❦❦❦ BORAX AND MEAL

*Recipe #1.* 3 parts borax (from supermarket laundry supply); 10 parts white cornmeal; 3 tablespoons salt.

*Recipe #2.* 1 part borax; 1 part yellow cornmeal; 3 tablespoons salt.

COLORAMA *Within this symmetrical mass design, each silica-gel-dried bud and flower is placed to emphasize its neighbor, with luminous freesias in contrast to the brilliant red-orange Tropicana roses that dominate the design. All the various shapes of the flowers are knowingly displayed from full-front in the lower middle area shifting to profile views along the edge and at the top. Such placements develop a satisfying three-dimensional perspective.* Mrs. H. King, Pennsylvania.

[E. Gilchrist, Jr., photo]

JUNE'S FRAGRANCE LINGERS *Holding the form and scent of freshly gathered blooms, these three sunshine-yellow roses with their own dried foliage are a nostalgic reminder of summer to be enjoyed through the length of winter. Leaves, stems, and flowers are dried individually in silica gel, carefully reassembled with wire and tape, and then arranged in the cream-and-gold vase. This piece is romantic in every aspect, from the French Victorian container to the selection and placement of the roses in a simple triangular design.* Mrs. J. Wilson, Canada.

[C. Webster photo]

Borax used alone cakes badly and may remove moisture so fast that petals burn. Meal alone may attract insects that feast on the medium and flowers alike. Since borax quickly draws moisture, the quantity used in your mixture will influence the drying time needed. Watch carefully, as a flower left even a day too long will lose color brilliance in any medium. Red flowers should not be treated in meal, as the dust is difficult to remove. Do not use borax mixtures in metal containers; never cover during the drying time.

### ❧❧❧ BORAX AND SAND

*Recipe #1* (Heavy Sand). 3 parts borax; 1 part clean, fine, sifted sand. Mix thoroughly. Ingredients must be dry.

*Recipe #2* (Light Sand). 1 part borax; 3 parts sand. Mix thoroughly. Ingredients must be dry.

*Recipe #3.* 15 pounds washed sand. Place in 350-degree F. oven until heated through. Add 3 tablespoons melted paraffin and stir thoroughly until wax is evenly distributed through the sand. Cool, add 1 tablespoon soda and 1 tablespoon borax or fine white silica gel. Stir thoroughly through the sand-wax mixture.

Some hobbyists feel a more natural gloss and texture are retained in sand than by any other drying process. Sand alone works slowly (three weeks) and is often too weighty for the more fragile flower tissues. However, flowers may be left in it indefinitely without injury. Sand may be dug or purchased from builders' supply sources. It must be clean, salt-free, and dry. The grains must be fine and round to avoid pitting the petals with large, sharp points. Do not cover the container when processing. Drying time requires two to three weeks.

### ❧❧❧ KITTY LITTER

Kitty Litter obtained from supermarkets is a successful substitute for sand or granular mixes; it is inexpensive and lightweight. Use the same methods as for other granular mixes. Time needed is approximately the same as for borax-sand.

# LIQUID TREATMENTS

*Recipe #1* (Stem Absorption). ⅓ glycerin or antifreeze; ⅔ hot water; 2 tablespoons laundry bleach, Lysol, or rubbing alcohol per cup of solution to reduce bacteria, molds; food coloring (optional) may enrich greens.

*Recipe #2* (Leaf Immersion). 1 part glycerin or antifreeze; 1 part warm water; 2 tablespoons bleach, Lysol, or rubbing alcohol per cup of glycerine mixture; food coloring (optional).

Liquid treatment preserves the natural three-dimensional form of plant materials but with a sacrifice of color stability in many cases. Colors after treatment by antifreeze are often not so rich as with glycerin.

### ❧❧❧ STEM ABSORPTION

Many purchased leaves and branches that are still fresh enough to absorb liquid through their stems can be easily preserved. The solution will be absorbed more readily if the foliage is cut after a dry spell during summer heat and when the leaf is mature. Select well-shaped branches about 18 inches long, crush the ends, and warm the solution for fast absorption. Don't despair if the tip leaves do not completely process. Remove them and carefully wire properly conditioned leaves of graduated sizes in their place.

During processing the leaves need plenty of air circulation. Since glycerin is rather expensive, a neat practical way is to drill holes partway through a 2-inch-thick board to accommodate large test or orchid tubes. It takes only two to three tablespoons of solution to fill the tube, plus the stem; leaves are not crowded, and the board is easily moved and stored.

Before placing in solution and at least once daily thereafter, rub a solution-soaked cloth over both sides of heavy leaves. This prevents excessive edge-drying and keeps leaves pliable until liquid has time to rise inside.

Foliage may be removed any time the color appeals. If removed after one week, some leaves may be brown in the center with irregular green outlines at the edges. Such leaves keep well and make interesting design additions. Experiment by placing in full sun or dark room during processing. Results will vary surprisingly.

Thin-textured materials that do not change color require less time to process and should be more closely watched to decide when enough is enough. Too much absorption makes leaves limp; hang upside down for ten days to return to normal. A week is usually needed even for fine-textured types.

FIGURE 27

Liquid-treated leaves keep almost indefinitely and remain pliable. Since water does not harm them, they may be used in fresh designs with no additional protection. Any leftover solution should be stored in a covered jar and may be reused. If it scums or mildews, simply skim and strain before using. Darkening does no damage to its effectiveness.

## ❦❦❦ LEAF IMMERSION

Boston and English ivies, as well as other groundcovers and plants that absorb moisture through their leaves, should be immersed completely in solution for two to six days. Weight leaves to hold under the liquid. Drain on newspapers. Hosta, lily-of-the-valley, violets, ivy, and galax will remain green and pliable.

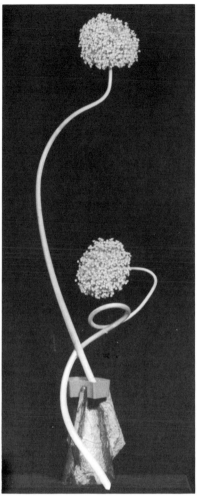

GEMINI *Here, in defiance of the old rule of three, two heads of natural dried allium take flight, extending focal interest over the whole in the manner of abstract designing. In this creative handling, the lower stem bypasses the cup pinholder and the inverted container (covered with green tissue paper) to rest firmly on the tabletop. The understatement of this design is emphasized by the use of a single plant type. Mrs. W. Wilson, South Carolina.*

[*Van Moore photo*]

# AIR-DRYING

Hanging, standing, and natural methods are the three main processes involved in air-drying. These are the oldest, simplest, and easiest ways of preserving plant materials. In the case of most blooms, however, considerable shrinkage and color alteration result. All drying should take place in an airy, warm, dry, dark spot. Attics and warm furnace rooms are usually ideal. Garages and basements are often too damp. Place in perforated brown paper bags that help retain color as well as keep the dust off during processing.

## ❦❦❦ HANGING

Some foliages and small compact double blooms, most pods and grasses dry well by the old-fashioned method of hanging head down. Flowers should be picked just before they reach maturity. If picked too soon, they wither; if picked on the wane, petals may fall or maturity will continue to seed development, thus ruining the form. It usually takes two to three weeks for most flowers to dry entirely.

A variation is to stick stems through a strip of 1-inch-mesh hardware cloth, leaving heads supported and stems hanging free. Some material will take on curved shapes useful in modern designing. While still soft and pliable, stems may be wired to curves or angles and then dried. Before hanging or standing, consider the natural form of the plant or of your intended design to determine how the plant should be positioned to retain or remake the shape during drying.

Some foliage will hang-dry into

weird, surrealistic shapes that are very usable for achieving form and depth in designs. Balsam-root, cocklebur, squash, strelitzia, horse-radish, banana, canna, and cecropia are examples.

### ✿✿✿ STANDING

Interesting curves can be created by standing echinops, poppy pods, bear grass, and many other types in containers of various heights. The lower the container, the more pronounced the droop before drying is complete. Dry some of the same types by hanging to have both straight and curved lines for your designs.

### ✿✿✿ NATURAL DRIED

Nature preserves some of the most exciting arrangement materials. Most pods, cones, lichens, fungus, seeds, and grasses need no more than gathering and mechanics to make them ready for your designs.

### ✿✿✿ PRESSING

Pressed flora have a definite place in the field of designing with dried plant materials. Flower pictures have long been popular, especially as memory pieces.

Place ferns, vines, foliages, or flowers on thick layers of newspaper (do not use slick paper), spreading out so none touches another, or they will stick together during drying and be impossible to separate without tearing. If it is necessary to overlap them, place pieces of absorbent toweling between the layers. Cover with more layers of newspaper and repeat for about six layers. Do not build too high a pile as it may get soggy and mold.

Weight with boards or books, making sure pressure is evenly distributed. Two to three weeks are needed, depending on the moisture content and humidity in your drying area. Gentle heat can be applied by directing a 10-watt bulb at the stack, or placing it on top of a television set or clothes dryer. Or place inside your warm clothes dryer, warning the family. It's pretty frustrating to find your papers and petals whipping around inside if someone accidentally turns on the machine. For special pressed curves, staple or tape (using hair tape) branches and fern fronds in desired curve to stiff cardboard before weighting between papers. Ferns may be steamed after pressing and their natural flexibility regained.

### ✿✿✿ PACKAGE PROCESS

A second method for pressing leaves that retains more of the natural form is to make small stacks, separating the leaves with a layer of absorbent toweling. Fasten the package loosely with string, tape, or staples. Do not weight. The less pressure, the more uneven the surface when dry, and the more the natural veins and textures will be preserved. Hosta, cocklebur, squash, lily-of-the-valley respond to this process. Pressed packaged leaves take about two to three weeks and may remain in the papers indefinitely without danger of fading.

Clean the foliage to be pressed by either method by wiping with a cloth dampened with olive or mineral oil or whole milk. Or spray with Plant Gloss.

# SPECIAL PROCESSES

### ❦❦❦ SPEED-DRYING WITH HEAT

You will find it is practical to dry more material than you anticipate using; even so, sometimes in making a design you may find a few more leaves or flowers of a certain type or color are quickly needed. The flowers are packed in a granular medium in the usual manner and the box placed over a furnace register or in a very low oven (100 degrees F.). Test a petal edge frequently, and as soon as it is crisp, remove; otherwise the blossoms will be too brittle to handle. Additional supported air-drying may be required for the calyx and stem (see Placing in Chapter 8). In areas of high humidity, broad-petaled flowers (gladiolus, lilies) need additional heat to dry properly. White flowers usually dry whiter if processed with a bit more heat.

Lily-of-the-valley and hosta leaves dry to perfection in an oven set at 150 degrees F. for twenty to thirty minutes. Gently wipe both sides of leaves and stems with cloth dipped in olive oil. Place in a single layer on a cookie sheet. Leave uncovered. If stems are not completely dry in half an hour, remove anyway, as they will continue to dry without shriveling in the open air. Leaves processed in this way are brilliant green with a lifelike sheen.

### ❦❦❦ SKELETONIZING

You have undoubtedly admired those misty ethereal leaves seen at flower shows and in florist's designs. They are not something new, but a process revived from Grandmother's day. Though they look delicate, skeletonized leaves are quite durable and hold their shape very well. While it is possible to skeletonize your own leaves, it's a tedious job requiring a delicate but firm touch. It's far simpler to keep on hand a few purchased tinted or bleached leaves from your florist. For those who, because of the challenge, or to meet a flower-show requirement, want to do their own, here are two successful processes.

*Recipe #1.* 2 tablespoons lye mixed into 1 quart water. Add leaves. Boil 15 minutes to 1 hour in an enamel or Pyrex pan. Then place in a mixture of half vinegar and half water while you brush off the fleshy parts with a dull knife or old toothbrush. Wash under running water.

*Recipe #2.* 1 teaspoon soda, 1 quart water. Boil leaves 30 to 60 minutes. Cool in the solution. Scrape away fleshy parts, working carefully to avoid tearing the webbing.

Leaves can also be skeletonized by boiling in detergent and water until nothing but the veining remains. Cool leaves in solution. The final mellow ivory color may be altered by tinting in hot fabric dye or by spraying. Take care to hold the can at a distance to avoid clogging the lacy vein patterns.

Use skeletonizing recipe #1 or #2 on magnolia, avocado, prickly-pear cactus (both round pad and cow's-tongue), rhododendron, ti, croton, and salal. Use # 1 for foliage types such as huckleberry, smilax, spiral eucalyptus, fern, spring rye, arborvitae, and galax. Singe the spines off cactus before boiling. One advantage of doing your own leaves is that you have a much wider choice of shape and size.

Skeletonized leaves may be dipped in glycerin to keep them pliable. Most heavy leaves that glycerinize satisfactorily may skeletonize as they age during storage. To purposely accomplish this, place one leaf over the next, wrap the stack in wax paper to retain any moisture, and store in a damp place six months. The fleshy parts will disintegrate and can be removed by light touches with a soft brush. More depth can be added to skeletonized leaves by dampening, curling, and fastening them until again dry.

## ❧❧❧ CRYSTAL-DIPPING

Heads of wild parsley become scintillating rays; each barley bristle becomes diamond-beaded, reflecting many colors, glittering, unreal; dried pods, grasses, and weeds are transformed as if by a fairy hand when crystal-dipped.

*Recipe.* 1 pound rock alum (drugstore); 1 quart water; vegetable coloring (optional, grocery store). Place alum and water in a container wide enough to accommodate the plant material. Heat until alum is dissolved. Cool slightly. Thrust a wire sideways through the stems to suspend with pods or heads below the solution, which, as it cools, forms crystals on the plant material. Watch closely when crystals begin to form, as their

size is determined by the solution strength (which may be varied to your liking) and the length of time materials are processed.

FIGURE 28

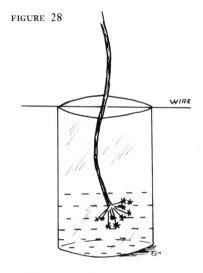

WIRE

When crystals are the right size for the scale of the material and the strength of stem (crystals are heavy), remove from the solution. Place each stem in a block of Styrofoam or a can of sand, keeping stems separated until dry. If not kept apart, the crystals will meld and be impossible to separate without breaking. Crystals are loosely attached and the material must be gently handled.

The crystallizing solution may be tinted with food coloring. Red and blue make a lovely delicate red-violet when white-sprayed pods are dipped into it. The dried material, both stem and pods, may be sprayed (same or different colors) before crystal-dipping, and they will absorb the color with interesting results. Wild parsley heads and stems sprayed flat black and dipped into untinted solution become a crystaled, white-topped form that is guaranteed to stop traffic. Select rough or textured, spiked or bearded pods and heads, as the crystals do not readily cling to flat, large, smooth surfaces. The solution may be reused by simply reheating. Will not damage metal kettles.

### ❦❦❦ GLASSING DRIED FLOWERS

Flowers of substantial substance (roses) can be dipped into Dippity Glas to give a heavy crystallike appearance. Spray allium or wild parsley brilliant colors, then dip into Dippity Glas for exciting variations. If working with flowers of less substance (azaleas, etc.), spray with several heavy coats of Spray-Glaze (Tandy) for a unique glasslike appearance. Or S. F. Clear Glue can be spread on petals (as evening primrose) to get the same effect. This takes time and patience but the color remains unchanged and the petals flexible with no shrinking.

### ❦❦❦ POMANDER BALLS WITH DRIED FLOWERS

Select apples, lemons, or oranges. Push a double row of whole cloves (which are preservatives) in at the stem end, add a row of bright star everlastings, another row of cloves, and continue alternating rows until the fruit is entirely covered, with no skin showing. Sprinkle crushed orris root or powdered cloves on the clove heads, avoiding the flowers. Thrust a brown or colored chenille wire into the stem end. Hang to dry four weeks.

### ❦❦❦ ENAMELING FRESH FLOWERS

Imagine the delighted surprise of your favorite bride if you present her with a jewel box decorated with enameled stephanotis, roses, or orange blossoms from her own bride's bouquet, an endearing memento to cherish through the years. Your magic wand is a very small camel's-hair artist's brush dipped into quick-drying enamel. Enamel in spray cans is less controllable, and you still need the brush to shape petals as the paint dries. Very small fruits, tiny bunches of berries, leaves, small double and single flowers from memory bouquets can be glued to surfaces or if heavy, wired for use in plaque work. Cloth and lace can also be enameled and glued for collage effects or trims on jewel boxes.

Apply white enamel to top surface of petal first, shaping as it dries. Repeat on the lower surface. Apply three coats, allowing each to dry completely before applying the next. The fourth enamel coat is the color you wish. The trick in enameling is to build coats smoothly to get a velvety-smooth, ceramic-like surface so perfect it is a mirrored reflection of the original bloom.

### ❦❦❦ WAXING FRESH AND FAKE FLOWERS

Pearlizing fresh and fake flowers and fruits by wax-dipping was a common household art in Grandmother's day and one which enjoys periodic revivals, as it yields some interesting material for home decoration. Fresh waxed flowers last about ten days, though their life will be extended if kept under apothecary jars, Victorian bells, or hurricane chimneys. They may be sprayed or porcelainized when brown.

Crepe paper, fabric, fresh fruits, and sasanqua camellias, small double camellias, buddleias, shasta daisies, gardenias, and larkspur are enormously successful. Choose flowers only in white or pastel.

If of fabric or paper, hold the flower under the wax until saturated. Remove. Shake off excess wax on a newspaper. Shape by separating, opening, and curling petals. Plunge directly into a deep bowl of ice water (cubes removed). A contrary petal can be resoftened and reshaped by holding close to a warm burner. Apply several coats to achieve the pearlized effect. Leftover candles or crayons can be used instead of wax or with it for color.

## ❧❧❧ PORCELAIN FINISH FOR FLOWERS (PLASTIC AND WAXED)

*Recipe #1.* 1 cup turpentine; 1 cup oak stain; 2 tablespoons gilt. Mix in a coffee can.

*Recipe #2.* ¼ cup clear varnish; ½ cup turpentine; ¼ teaspoon dark oak stain; ½ teaspoon bronze powder.

Dip the flower in solution #1 or #2. Shake hard, and drain on wire screening 24 hours. The secret

FRUIT BOWL *Common garden produce is treated here to simulate marble in a semipermanent design that emphasizes forms rather than colors or the space in which objects exist. Fruit, leaves, and cones are all sprayed with six coats of white enamel. The simple horizontal placement and restrained selection of forms contribute to a feeling of unstudied elegance. Marie O'Connor, Oregon.* [*D. Kettler photo*]

is to shake well; work outdoors to protect furniture. Use a small paintbrush to reach places on stems. Keep gilt or bronze suspended by stirring as you work. The solution softens colors that are garish and gives each flower unique highlights. A pink rose comes out a delicate dusky hue and plastic flowers appear sheer rather than thick. Many other items (plastic fruit, dried flowers, gourds, baskets, decorative wood) can be transformed by this process.

## ❦❦❦ EMBEDDING IN PLASTIC

Herbs, grasses, pods, berries, flowers, ferns, twigs, bamboo circles are but a few of the dried things that can be embedded in plastic for use in screens, room dividers, paperweights, key chains, coasters, trays, place mats, and switch plates. Materials are available in kits from hobby shops. Casto-glas is one popular brand that comes with complete instructions.

# SEMIPERMANENT PROCESSES

## ❦❦❦ VARNISHED LEAVES

Deep winter usually brings a wish to use fresh foliages. You can make one investment last several months by brushing or spraying rubber plant, laurel, magnolia, fiddleleaf fig, croton, and dracaena foliage with clear white dammar varnish, like that used by artists to preserve their paintings.

## ❦❦❦ SPRAY-WAXED FOLIAGE AND FLOWERS

Spray wax (Florawax) will extend foliage and flower life amazingly. Foliage coated on both sides will stay fresh-looking several months even without water. This spray produces no noticeable change in the appearance of flowers or foliage except on red roses, which may blue slightly. Be sure materials are dry before application.

## ❦❦❦ ALCOHOL-SHELLACKING FOR

## BERRIES, PODS

*Recipe.* 1 cup white shellac; 1 cup wood alcohol or alcohol-based solvent. Pour into a shallow pan and dip the materials, using a 1- to 2-inch artist's brush to assure complete coverage. Handle outdoors or in a well-ventilated room. Hang-drip until dry. Keep surplus solution tightly closed during storage.

Hard berries such as bayberry are most successful for enduring use. The life expectancy of mountain ash and pyracantha berries, even when shellacked, is shorter, as they will eventually shrivel. Individual pricking of each berry with a needle allows internal drying and aids the preservation process. A shellac-alcohol treatment will brighten age- or weather-dulled cones and pods.

Spraying with clear plastics and varnishes is effective but you may feel the thicker coating gives a less natural appearance. Such sprays can be used to make colors of borax-meal-dried flowers come to life. Superhold hair sprays and clear Flora-Set give non-shine support and durability to fragile seed heads like meadow salsify (goatsbeard).

## ❧❧❧ LONGER-LASTING EVERGREENS

*Recipe #1.* 1 gallon hot water; 4 tablespoons micronized-iron plant food; 2 cups light corn syrup; 4 teaspoons chlorinated household bleach.

Split or pound 2 inches of stem ends, and immerse in the mixture. Add more liquid daily as it evaporates. Leave stem ends in solution at least 3 days. This preserves evergreens (both needle and broadleaf) for extended periods without foliage drop or discoloration.

*Recipe #2.* 1 quart hot water; 1 cup Karo syrup; 1 teaspoon Clorox bleach.

Use as directed for Recipe # 1.

*Recipe #3* (recommended for hollies). ½ pound brown sugar; 2 quarts hot water.

Use as directed for # 1.

*Recipe #4* (recommended for boxwood). First immerse in cold water 6 hours. Remove to pail and add 1 quart hot water, 1 teaspoon laundry bleach, 1 teaspoon powdered sugar. Let stand until water cools before using.

*Recipe #5* (fire-deterrent solution for evergreens and dried materials). 4 ounces boric acid; 9 ounces borax; 1 gallon water.

Fire-deterrent solution for evergreens and drieds may be required for flower shows, and could avert a home tragedy. Spray or dip. Seals moisture in fresh foliage and out of drieds.

## ❧❧❧ DRY STORAGE

One of the most eye-catching arrangements at a June show did not owe attention entirely to the creativity of the designer, but to the fact that the pink tulips in it had been picked from the arranger's own garden in March!

The dry storage method is also a great help to the design exhibitor of specialty shows. Dry storage spreads the gathering of cut flowers over several days, giving each exhibitor in the family a better chance at choice blooms.

Roses, peonies, daffodils, and other flowers can be easily and successfully preserved in dry storage. Clean the foliage while the flower remains on the recently watered bush. Cutting should be done in late afternoon when one to three petals start to unfurl and the calyx is loosening. If the rose or peony is very double, let three or four petals open; cutting earlier often results in failure to open, and letting more petals unfurl often results in greater loss of substance.

Wrap flowers carefully in Pliofilm and lay in plastic bags with heads supported. Place in a refrigerator (a spare one is a godsend), set at 33 degrees F. (normal refrigerator temperature is 40 to 42 degrees F.). About eight hours before needed, remove from refrigerator. Leaving blooms wrapped, turn back the Pliofilm to expose stem ends. With a diagonal slash, cut ¾ inch off each stem. Place in 2 inches of hot water (106–110 degrees F.) for twenty minutes. Transfer to cool water for six to eight hours of continued conditioning in a cool dark place. Let the Pliofilm remain over the blooms and upper stems during the entire process. Don't be shocked at the wilted appearance when you place in hot water; the flowers will revive. Reds may show some bluing; pastels and whites have the most color stability. There may be some loss of substance and natural petal sheen, but dry-stored flowers have won ribbons even in the horticultural cut-flower section of plant-society shows. Experiment with the types and varieties you grow, for not all respond the same way.

# COLOR ALTERATION

While purists will object to color alteration, taking justified pride in emphasizing the preservation of natural hues, still, realistically speaking, there are a number of occasions when color touch-ups or downright dyeing save the day. Your flower border, florist, or drying room may not always be able to deliver the right color to complement fabrics, china, interior decoration, or a specific design situation. Also, age can dull a dried flower though the form is still perfect.

When making designs to compete in a flower show, check the schedule rules carefully to see if color-altered plant materials are allowed. In abstract designing where line, form, texture, and color are used purely for their contribution to the design, with little or no regard for naturalness, color altering is often a great advantage.

## ❧❧❧ SPRAY-PAINTING

More natural effects will be achieved if the form of the flower is compatible with the color of spray paint used. It is normal to see red roses or gladiolus, but a bright-red daffodil is a shock unless that is what is intended. Summer's yellow marigold or golden glow or white aster becomes Christmas's vivid red carnation with a can of red spray paint to make the change. While asters, marigolds, and golden glow are never red by nature, yet their forms are similar to the round carnation and therefore quite acceptable, yes, even unnoticeable! Pods and seed heads, branches, and decorative wood are more readily accepted without comment when altered to wild and unnatural colors. Reds that have dried a disappointing grayed shade can be revived to bright life by careful spraying.

Floral sprays (Gard's Spra-Tone) are light, airy, flower-color-matched in a full range and fast-drying, and they will not melt Styrofoam. Surfaces may be moist when sprayed. Spray by drifting the color down from 4 feet above, or coat heavily. For heavy applications hold the can 10 to 18 inches away to avoid dripping or blasting delicate petals from their moorings.

For psychedelic effects, different hues may be overlaid either before or after the first one is dry. Try pink with a dusting of yellow, purple with a drift of avocado; a whisk of another color relieves grim greens. A light dusting of "moss" over "spring" green gives interesting color depth. Experiment for extra color zip.

## ❧❧❧ DYEING

There are two dyeing processes: stem absorption and dip. White and pastel flowers respond best. In using stem absorption (Tintex), keep fresh flowers out of water until limp, then recut stems and stand in warm dye. Process may take twenty hours so flowers must be fresh, and less than mature. Carnations, daffodils, daisies, narcissus, and sweet peas respond nicely. Pat stems dry before placing in granular drying medium.

To dip-dye, use No-Rinse Dip or cold-water dye as recommended on the package. Process takes from a few minutes to an hour. Be sure flowers are completely dry before placing in medium. A few hours uncovered in the refrigerator will help draw off moisture. Experiment with dip-dyeing dried pods and fungi in very hot solutions of Tintex and No-Rinse Dip. Artichokes and yucca heads placed in hot orange Tintex turn a lovely copper shade.

## ❧❧❧ SHOE POLISH

Give the color of last season's liquid-treated or dried foliages a lift with common shoe polish. Intensify or alter to meet design needs. White polish on air-dried cocklebur gives a completely new look, especially if you do one side white, the other brown or black. Dampen the leaf under water for a few minutes until limp, apply polish, hang to dry. Brown polish revives magnolia and laurel, black deepens aucuba and pear, oxblood revitalizes beech and can be used to intensify or establish a russet tinge on many foliages. Mix food coloring with white shoe polish for unusual effects.

# 8 · Permanence Begins with Craft Techniques

"Perfection is no trifle but trifles make perfection," Michelangelo remarked four centuries ago, and today success also begins with craftsmanship, attention to the details of gathering at the proper time, having supplies on hand, proper placement in the medium, and removal, wiring, taping, and the right mechanics. Proper gluing, stem-extending, shaping, and grooming, as well as transporting and storage, are all important.

## GATHERING AND SELECTION TECHNIQUES

Generally speaking, flowers should be picked just as they reach or are about to reach their full color and beauty of form. Since maturity often continues for some hours after gathering, flowers picked after they have reached prime are more apt to shatter after drying. However, if some do shatter, don't panic—you can use the petals, stems, and leaves on stationery, in pictures, even for potpourri.

The maturity of fresh flowers influences the dried appearance. Flowers in which stamens and pollen can be observed (single roses, peonies, etc.) should show bright yellow pollen, no browning or dropping, and no shrinking of anthers. Marigolds and zinnias must have reached full maturity or they will shrink and you will be unpleasantly aware of the oversized seed area. Double flowers are freshest when the petals are crisp without thinning or browning of edges on both front and back. Flowers grown in good soil with proper attention to culture and watering will dry better than poorly grown flowers, as they will have superior petal substance.

Don't gather after a heavy shower or dew, or on humid days, for then you will have more moisture to remove to complete the dehydration process.

Don't pick on an extremely hot

day, as the petals become limp and cannot support the weight of the medium. Wilted fresh flowers can be rejuvenated in warm water (100 to 110 degrees F.) and left several hours in a dark place before you inter them in the granular medium. It doesn't matter if you must hold flowers for a few hours in water before granular-drying; just be sure stems have been patted dry with a soft cloth before you bury them.

Discard insect-chewed or damaged leaves or flowers unless the area can be trimmed away. Starting with perfect specimens is important, as preservation does not conceal; rather, it highlights blemishes.

When you go into the fields for salsify puffs and other plants to dry, carry cans of paint and also a clear plastic spray. Spray grasses and pods as they stand, tie a bright piece of yarn to stems as you proceed so you can readily find them again after they dry. If you want colored materials, apply the paint also as they stand on the plant. It's rather startling for passing motorists to see these "new" colored flowers but it does prevent shattering of fragile materials.

Good design is most important in dried arrangements, as the results last a season or more; so plan to gather or plant to suit certain containers, room color schemes, or locations in your home. Such planning adds an extra dimension to your horticultural experiences.

Harvest plenty of flowers along with an abundant supply of background and foliage materials. Develop an eye for "line" things so necessary to lift your dried designs above the cliché-type bouquets. Select light colors and pastels such as whites, pinks, yellows, also orange-reds and light blue, as most colors tend to darken in the drying process.

## SUPPLIES

Good work requires the right tools. Keep these in a special kit labeled *Drying Equipment*. Since drying is a continuing thing from spring through fall, your tools should be handy at any time a perfect bloom presents itself.

Essential supplies include:
small sharp scissors with long, narrow blades
pruning shears, long-nosed pliers with wire-cutting edge
razor blades (cover one edge with tape to protect fingers or get single-edge type)
tapes (adhesive, florist's, magic, tacky, Scotch, mystic, masking)

pins (straight sewing and fine wire-like insect-mounting pins obtainable from university botany supply stores
fruitcake, nut, or other cans with tight covers for silica gel drying
open containers, boxes for granular processing that need no seal
jars and containers for liquid absorption methods
camel's-hair or sable artist's brushes in several sizes
glue, a good, fast, and clear-drying one
toothpicks, staples, stapler, wire, stem-extenders
clay (floral, modeling, and plaster of paris)

MINUET   *A feeling for the romantic and feminine delicacy of the time of Marie Antoinette is evident here in the choice of delicate pastel roses, snapdragons, statice, larkspur, daisies, and green hydrangeas, all dried in pure white sand. The antique porcelain container enhances the fragile-appearing massed flowers, and a traditional spirit of sprightly grace is communicated. The emphasis is gloriously floral. Mrs. W. Busanus, Pennsylvania.*

[*P. Orner, Sr., photo*]

florist orchid tubes, Aqua-picks,
saw for cutting wood and branches
paraffin, plastic bags in various sizes,
rubber bands, newspapers
kitchen self-sealing Pliofilm, vases,
containers, holders
patience and stick-to-itiveness

# WIRING

I have been most successful in wiring
before drying. Wiring may seem to
be a fussy, unneeded task until you
find stems too brittle or weak-
necked to withstand even careful
handling during arranging.

You will find wired stems so much
more manipulative, going to whatever lengths you need, rather than
merely those nature provides. They
add stability and allow shaping in
the arrangement. It takes little extra
time once you have a bit of mechan-
ical know-how.

Wired, taped stems are often more
practical, too, when the finished
flower or leaf is used with fresh plant
material. The water needed to keep
the fresh blooms from wilting will
often soften the dried natural stem
to the point where it will not stand
on the holder, or moisture may even
invade the stem by capillary action,
causing staining and drooping.

Except for strawflowers, few air-
dried plants need wiring unless you
wish to shift the flowers or leaves
around. This often is the case with
lunaria and Chinese lantern, which
are both easier to work with if re-
clustered.

The gauges of wire can be confusing at first. The higher the gauge
the finer the wire.

#18 is quite stiff; use for large
dahlias, etc. You will also use #18
or #20 to lengthen stems and reassemble spikes.

#24 to 28 are medium; use for
clematis, daffodils, small dahlias, and
roses.

#30 to 32 are threadlike; needed
for pansies, violets, etc.

All are available from your florist
in 9-, 12-, 18-inch lengths. The finer
gauges are also found on spools.

There are several methods of at-
taching the wire. Which method to
use depends on the type of calyx
and the doubleness of the flower.

*Method #1*

The simplest attachment used on
any flower with a fairly heavy and
pithy-centered stem (rose) is to
remove all but ½ inch of the natural
stem. Insert a piece of medium-
weight wire into the stub and up
into the calyx. That's all. The stem
will shrink tight around the wire
during drying, clutching it almost
irremovably tight. This won't work
with all flowers. I just tried it on a
*Begonia phyllomaniaca*, which has a
large succulent stem; the wire
promptly fell out when the leaf was
removed from the media. However,
it clung inside the rex begonia leaves.

*Method #2—Hook Method*

After removing all but ½ inch of
the natural stem, push a medium-
gauge wire down through the center

FIGURE 29

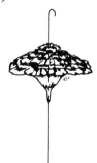

of the flower's face, guiding and pushing until it emerges at or near the stub of the stem. Before pulling all the way down through the flower face, turn over a ¼-inch hook on the upper end. Figure 29. Then carefully finish pulling until the hook nestles invisibly in the petals or throat and is firmly anchored. Chrysanthemums, strawflowers, calendulas, marigolds, asters, even snapdragons and gladiolus are a few of the types so wired.

*Method #3—Clutch Method*

This provides a double-wire stem approximately 9 inches long. Bend an 18-inch length of medium-gauge wire just short of the center. Place the short side on parallel with the natural stem, so the bend is as high as possible up under the flower head. Hold stem and wire firmly together, then, beginning where you bent the wire, twist the longer half around both the natural stem and the flower wire several times and bring ends all down together. Sometimes you will find the stem has shrunk and slips through after drying; if so, wrap with floral tape, rewire, and again tape.

FIGURE 30

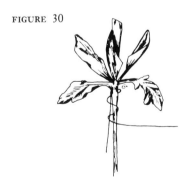

*Method #4—Bridling*

Some flowers—roses, daffodils, carnations—have heavy, tough ca-

FIGURE 31

lyxes and should be "bridled." Recut medium wire ends on a slant to sharpen enough to ease pushing. Push the 18-inch length horizontally through the green calyx until there is an equal length of wire on each side. Turn the flower halfway around and push through another 18-inch piece. Bring the wires down along the natural stem, stub and tape. (Figure 31.)

*Method #5—Inner Reinforcing*

Leave the natural hollow or pulpy stem (tulips, etc.) as long as when picked; push a heavy-to-medium wire through from the bottom of the stem. Push until the wire tip is secure in the base of the bloom. Gentle curving can be done with this method, and in the case of tulips, it keeps fresh ones from following the light.

Don't forget that you will want some buds for your designs. Use the bridling method for those of gladiolus, roses, etc.

*Foliage wiring—Stitch Method*

Foliage is necessary to most good designs and occasionally it must be restructured to make it usable. For perfect poise, position, and stability, we invisibly back-wire many tall vertical leaves, using an 18-inch length of medium-to-fine wire. Take a short stitch across the leaf's

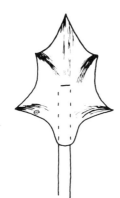

FIGURE 32

center rib about halfway up the back of the leaf. (Figure 32.) Bring one wire end all the way down parallel to the natural stem. Bring the other end down and twist around both the first end and the natural stem.

## ❧❧❧ REASSEMBLING VINES AND SPIKES

Small foliages, such as *Vinca minor* and ivy or huckleberry, are often cluster-structured on heavy wire "vines" to facilitate using in garlands, wreaths, and designs. After treating in Method #2 stitch-wire each leaf across the heavy center rib near the bottom of the leaf. Bring wire ends down, and Floratape each short length. Then, using a heavy to medium wire, tape a small leaf at the top and others at natural intervals, alternately reassembling into a flexible vine. Liquid-cured foliages can be stitch-wired and vined after processing, but I've found it less damaging to wire foliages to be granular-treated before processing.

Gladiolus, snapdragons, jonquils, triandrus and tazetta narcissus, to name only a few, grow on main stems that are heavy in comparison to the flowers. It is usually best, because of succulence, size, and shrinking of this main stem, to remove each floret and wire and reassemble the flowers. Since the lower end of both gladiolus and snapdragon florets are crisp and easily sliced through by the wire, first wrap the base with a bit of tape; then add a short wire, either by Hook Method #2 or Clutch Method #3. Next, select a longer, heavier wire to replace the natural main stem. Study the natural inflorescence (the way the flowers grow on the spike). For instance, gladiolus starts at the top with a tight bud, each lower bud and flower fits close to the main stem, while *Narcissus tazetta* has a much looser attachment and a longer stem for each individual floret. In the case of gladiolus, tape the first bud to the stem, add another close below, proceed down the main stem adding increasingly open florets with a continuous piece of tape, ending with your largest flower.

When reassembling spikes, space as on the natural stem or even closer. The advantage of reassembling over drying the natural stem is that widening of the spaces between flowers due to shrinking is avoided. But when you reassemble, you can place the florets in an ideal position to give a perfect effect, improving on nature if need be. Small leaves can be wired in a branchlike pattern to make them more obedient to the curving often required for a design. You can also make unusual new types of inflorescence for a common flower. For instance, assemble small zinnias, marigolds, azaleas, roses in a tight gladiolus-like spike, and curve it to use as a line or cascade in your design. Experiment and review Chapter 6 on contrived forms.

## GLUING

The optimistic craftsman is happy over the fine new glues available; the pessimist thinks it only proves more things are falling apart. Be that as it may, a good, fast, and clear-drying adhesive is a necessity for reinforcing and replacing petals. A white creamy one, such as Elmer's Glue or S. F. Clear, will not stain flower petals if the glue is entirely dry when flowers are placed in the medium. If not dry, there is sometimes a chemical reaction that causes spotting.

Gluing is both a pre-dry and post-dried operation. You will have fewer casualties if you get in the good habit of applying a few drops of glue to every flower you process of the types most apt to shatter. Clematis, bells-of-Ireland, field daisies, chrysanthemums are among the worst offenders.

Candle wax can be dripped down into a rose center and between the petals; squeeze lightly until set in tighter bud form if wished. Spray or drip wax on backs of chrysanthemums for shatter prevention.

## PLACING IN MEDIUM

Each flower's characteristic form dictates the special handling and placement in the preservative. Care should be taken when using granular methods to keep the petals in as natural a position as possible so as to retain characteristic form. Practice will make you adept.

I've found pure sand too heavy for delicate clematis and hollyhocks; they need medium-weight silica gel or borax-cornmeal mixtures. A mixture of detergent and cornmeal is lightest of all and works well on the delicate flowers of evening primrose, potentilla, and violets. There is no crushing and less form distortion or pitting of petals when the proper weight medium is selected for the flower being dried. Be sure flowers are entirely dry; otherwise they may mold in the medium. Deeply cupped or throated flowers may be carefully stuffed with shredded absorbent paper toweling before being placed. This helps retain the natural shape of lilies, hemerocallis, daffodils, and orchids. Brace the orchid tube in the center of the flower and continue the bracing even after removal, as its length and weight often drags the tube to one side until the flower is completely dry. Do not use cotton in throats as the juices may cause sticking when the cotton is drawn from the tissues; then removal becomes difficult without damaging the flower.

To make your mixture go farther, bunched absorbent toweling may be placed around and under large flower clusters and stems before you drift the medium over them. Be sure that at least a ½-inch layer of medium is in direct contact with any petal.

### 🌷🌷🌷 BLEEDERS

Some plants—poinsettias, poppies, hollyhocks, and snow-on-the-mountain—bleed a white juice when freshly cut. Immediately sear the stems by holding them over the flame from a couple of tablespoons of rubbing alcohol in a small container. Cut these stems longer than the ½-inch stub recommended under Wiring. Sealing ends, even when drying such bleeders, results in a more lifelike bloom form. Roses also benefit from this treatment. Sealing can also be done over a lighted gas or electric burner or with a long fireplace match.

### 🌷🌷🌷 SEPARATING FLOWERS

Avoid placing different types of flowers in the same box, as drying times vary and blooms and stems may tangle, causing damage. Do not let flower petals overlap or you will surely damage one when removing the next. It is wisest to dry only one to three blooms of similar process-time, maturity, and type in each container.

### 🌷🌷🌷 FACE UP VERSUS . . .

Your goal is to contour-dry flowers so as to preserve natural forms. Almost all blossoms are more likelike if, during the drying process, they are placed face up in the position they grow in. Exceptions are spike types, such as delphinium, larkspur, etc., which are placed horizontally (Figure 34), and multiple-flowered heads, as lilac and hydrangea, which are hung in the medium (Figure 35).

FIGURE 33

When natural stems are retained, it's best in most cases to strip off the foliage and use the perforated-bottom-type box discussed below (Figure 37). If wire stems are substituted, bend the wire sharply up straight past the petals. It will stick out of the medium and help you locate the flower for removal (Figure 33).

If you prefer to dry flowers face down on the natural stems, be even more careful to preserve the form. Drying face down is more difficult, as you cannot see how you are progressing, and more flowers will come out unnaturally flattened. Place at least 1 inch of granular medium in the bottom of the container. Place the cups of single flowers face down over a mound of medium, and let the natural stem rest against the container side. It is not necessary to cover stems.

Careful covering of petals at this point is the technique that results in a natural-looking finished product. First a bit of the medium is shoved under the lower petals, then a bit sifted gently into the center as you guide and shape the flower. Continue spoon-pouring and working the medium until the entire flower is covered. You can shift and maneuver the petals of a single flower to achieve varying forms from bud to fully open by the way you manipulate the medium.

## ❧❧❧ SPECIAL TREATMENTS

A special method is needed for heavy, long spikes to prevent petals from being flattened on one side. Make a cardboard or wire support bridge for buddleia, bridal-wreath, flowering quince, larkspur, delphinium, or lythrum by folding the entire length of a piece of cardboard 3 inches wide in half. Notch along the length at intervals, making the notches wide enough to hold the stem. They may be off-centered to curve the line. Make several bridges for each box so each spike is supported in several places.

FIGURE 34

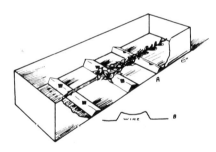

## ❧❧❧ DESIGNING AS YOU PLACE

You should try to imagine how you will be using the processed flowers since you cannot redo them. It's annoying to find all your lily-of-the-valley spikes swaying to the left when you need a few to bend to the right. Sometimes (as in making pictures with violets), you can snip the flower from the stem and turn the stem over as a remedy. Bend over the edges and tips of a few leaves as you place them to gain a more

natural three-dimensional look. Don't make the mistake of having all line materials sentinel-straight; curve a few stems. Spike types can be gently shaped by molding to a curved piece of #18 or lower-gauge wire.

To gently curve types that have no flowers or leaves on the back (silver-lace vine, ivy), lay flat in an empty box (no medium yet). Wire and tape the main stem directly to the bottom of the box in a gentle flowing curve. Cover with medium.

## ❧❧❧ LARGE-HEADED FLOWERS

A single large truss or head, such as hydrangea or lilac, dried on the natural stem, should be supported so the weight and that of the medium do not deform the individual fragile florets or distort the mounded or oval form of the entire head. Use a two-pound coffee can or one-gallon round cardboard ice-cream carton. Place 1 inch of medium in the bottom. Thrust a #18 wire horizontally through or wrap around the natural stem and lay wire across the container top, suspending the flower head in the carton (Figure 35). To

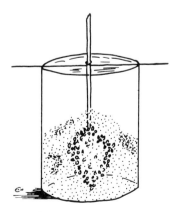

FIGURE 35

FIGURE 36

save medium when placing flowers face up, place Styrofoam 1 inch thick over the bottom (Figure 36). Use the can's own lid, or cover with Pliofilm and tape edges.

### ❧❧❧ RETAINING NATURAL STEMS

If you wish to keep the natural stems on a number of small flowers to be dried in granular mix, use a shallow box with a firm bottom; reinforce if necessary. Punch holes in the bottom far enough apart so the heads will not touch and big enough for stems to slide through easily, but not so

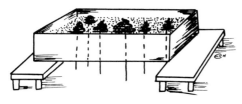

FIGURE 37

large that the medium sifts out; if it does, line the bottom with aluminum foil. Prop the box on edges of two benches so the stems hang free. Poke flower stems through holes, leaving the flower base resting on the box bottom; cover with medium. (Figure 37.)

### ❧❧❧ CHECKING PROGRESS

Check your boxes about twelve to eighteen hours after burial. The relaxing petals, especially of doubles, may allow the settling of medium leaving "toes" exposed. After a few hours or days, depending on total suggested processing time, brush aside a little of the medium to test petals for that crisp touch that indicates dryness.

### ❧❧❧ LABELING

Masking tape makes a quick container label, easily removed. Print information while still on the roll, and carefully label each container as to plant material, date, and medium. Keep these labels when uncovering and simply transfer them to the ends of your storage containers.

### ❧❧❧ PROTECTING LIQUID-DRIEDS AND AIR-DRIEDS

The processes of liquid treatment and air-drying often take weeks, so protect your plants from dust and fading by covering with a brown paper bag.

HANDLING FLOWERS FOR DRYING  ABOVE, LEFT: *A stem is elongated by wiring as in Method #1, page 100.* ABOVE, RIGHT: *Flowers are placed in a box of the drying agent.* BELOW, RIGHT: *The container of silica gel is sealed with tape.* BELOW, LEFT: *Processed flowers are stored in a closed jar. Flower-Dri Photos, Courtesy Planttab Corporation.* [*Valley Studios*]

# REMOVAL FROM MEDIUM

Since humidity and petal turgidity affect drying speed, it's impossible to give definite times to fit every situation. This is no time to be inept. Flick away some of the granular medium with an artist's brush and test the edge of a petal with the tip of your finger. Do not remove too soon; if you do, the flower will shrink and take on a crumpled look when exposed to air. A texture similar to taffeta and a rustling sound indicate petal dryness. But this is not to say the whole specimen is entirely dry. Stems, calyxes and buds of some temperamental types (tulips, narcissus, hollyhocks, etc.) may need more time. However, if the dry petals are left too long, the whole flower will tend to fall apart and will have increased brittleness and fragility as well as loss of color through natural leaching.

So remember, when the petals feel crisp, the flower is usually ready to be removed. At this point, uncover and finish the drying process by allowing the specimen to lie on top of the medium for another two to three days, at no risk to the petals already processed. Slowly expose the flowers by whisking away medium. Rarely will a flower break if you proceed carefully and with patience despite an almost uncontrollable desire to see how well all have turned out. Don't panic if some flowers shatter; side-line them for later use in collages, pressed pictures, and contrived forms. Or, if the damage is slight, take "patches" from other damaged flowers of the same kind, and color and glue to the backs of the torn petals.

# TAPING

Your decorative drieds are going to be on stage for considerable lengths of time, so take a few extra careful minutes to conceal the wires. Substitute wire stems, neatly taped, are almost indistinguishable from the real thing if care is taken to select floral tape of a near-natural color. I tape after drying, as there are bound to be failures—so why waste tape until you are sure of the results?

Floratape is a stretchy plastic product sold under various trade names and available at florist and hobby shops. It may be spray-painted after use, but is offered in many colors; green is natural for most flowers, while brown is best for most woody stems, such as dogwood. White or gray is good with gray foliages and for bleached and skeletonized leaves. The slick glossy type of white tape soils less easily than the grainy-surfaced kind. Black looks stunning on stems of pear, aucuba, and black-sprayed leaves. Lunaria (money-plant) dollars are dramatic when restructured on a heavier black-taped stem. Masking or freezer tape can be used as a substitute; it's a natural-appearing neutral tan color, sticks under water, and will not resist paint, as does transparent Scotch tape.

There's no trick to taping, but practice makes you feel less "all-thumbsy." The tape fortunately clings to itself which aids the process. Avoid stretching too tightly as it gets stringy and loses its grip and elasticity.

Grasp the tape and stem in your left hand as high up under the flower head as you can. Pinch tape and stem (or wire) with the left thumb and forefinger. Still holding in the left hand, and guiding with right thumb and forefinger, slowly and slightly stretch the tape in a bias position while slowly twirling the stem with your left hand. Spiral down to the stem end. Don't bother to cut; merely tear tape off the roll. For economy's sake, work with the tape attached to the roll. The finished stem should have a snug, smooth-fitting covering, slanted down its length. Don't pull or twirl too fast or you will have patches of wire showing. During the whole opera-

FIGURE 38

tion, hold the flower by the stem, not the head, or you'll end up with a headless well-taped stem! If your first attempt is loose or gaping, merely add another layer. Raffia (natural color) can be used as a substitute to tie, hold, and wrap stems, as its texture and color melt into that of many dried plants.

## STEM-EXTENDING

Though the taped-wire substitute stem is barely visible even in line designs, wire can be avoided in many instances by using what I call "natural stem extenders."

Any hollow or pithy stem can be utilized. Stems of cattail, larkspur, globe-thistle, bamboo stakes, Siberian iris, gladiolus and honeysuckle are some I have found that may be used either green or air-dried, and can be kept on hand to use when needed. Be careful to select stems that are properly proportioned to the size of the flower to be mounted. Heavy and thick stems supporting dainty flowers will never appear natural.

To use hollow stem extenders, just thrust the short wire of the flower (attached before drying) down into the pithy center. Remove and dribble glue into the hole and reset the wire. For a hollow stem, poke a few slim stems (wheat is fine for this) in around the wire stem of the flower to take up any excess play, then drip glue into the cavity. Seat the flower base firmly on top of the extender stem to encourage the impression of a natural joint. Make stems longer by overlapping a piece of natural stem on the substitute wire stem (which may need padding), and tape.

### ❧❧❧ SPECIAL SITUATIONS

Stemless flowers can be glued directly to properly scaled twigs and branches. Dogwood is effective this way and I contrived a new shrub by gluing yellow evening primroses on a graceful branchlike twig. If you find the stems of dainty flowers too short, stick them into clear drinking straws, trimming the straws to varying lengths. Clear straws will not be noticeable even in glass containers.

Fruits and vegetables and some pods are unwieldy. Impale them on chopsticks, knitting needles, or sharpened sticks before arranging, to avoid a bunched-up look.

I have found that a natural-appearing taped stem can be achieved by wiring a short wire stem to a slightly curved dried twig or tree branch. Because long natural lotus stems are unavailable, I attach lotus pods to the tops of dormant poplar branches. Tape, molded smoothly over prominent leaf nodes and natural curves, makes the result undetectable as fake.

Sometimes the end of a much-used natural stem will splay out, becoming impossible to make stand in the pinholder. Take a couple of loose turns around the area with Floratape, poke a few smaller stems into the cavity, dribble in a bit of glue, and let set. The result will often be stronger than the original.

## CREATIVITY WITH CONTAINERS

A dried flower arrangement is long-lasting, so carefully select a container that is just right in color, shape, character, texture, and size.

The container is limited only by the arranger's ingenuity to see, experiment, and utilize whatever object is the most compatible to her design and her plant materials. Happily, the designer of drieds does not have to worry about containers for water.

What a container *is* doesn't matter; it's the appearance and suitability to the plants used and the location that are important. Forget that your medium is dried; if the color and texture are right, the result will be satisfactory. Don't timidly hesitate, asking "Has it been done before?" Do it.

Cost may be nil or many dollars. Arrangers used to humorously refer to anything costing over $25.00 as a "vahze," but the cost of an original free-form container may far exceed this.

Containers may be nothing more than a base with holder attached. They may be plant materials themselves—driftwood, gourds, bamboo tubes, and slices cut from tree trunks. They may be an artist's free-formed object with space (holes) in the body and many openings. They may be parts of machinery or functional objects temporarily confiscated from unexpected areas of the economy. The list is as endless as the vision of the designer; for instance, a modern design on a square Plexiglas kitchen cutting board covered with a square lucite wastepaper basket; the composition reflects current taste with Victorian practicality in the protective see-through covering reminiscent of the glass bell.

## ❧❧❧ CONTAINER TIPS

An incompatible color, glaze, or shape tends to minimize the importance of the design. Harmony and rhythm can be achieved by repeating container shape in plant material.

Curved containers are easier to make curved designs in.

Rugged straight lines are better in straight-sided containers.

A base of a related form, texture, and/or color under a container can lift it and give better proportions.

Textures can be repeated, as, for instance, a shiny container with glossy holly.

Earthy and muted colors are easiest to use.

A solid color may be chosen from a busy background of wallpaper or drapery to emphasize it in the design, making it stand out from the domineering background.

White containers should be unified with the design by using some white plant material.

Containers with heavily raised, harshly colored floral or figure motifs should be spray-painted one color, or with the main color of the motif used in the floral design.

# HOLDERS

Walter Gropius once said, "Art cannot be learned, but what can be learned are the skills of the hand and what can be acquired is knowledge. Genius likewise cannot be taught but every creative artist is the better for having a craftsman's training." And certainly a craftsman's training and techniques are an aid in making your happily-ever-after flowers behave, for no matter how beautifully you have preserved color and form, no design is good unless the holder does its job.

## ❧❧❧ MECHANICS

Mechanics are devices used to give support and stability and should either be a part of the design or concealed without detriment to it. Adding a petticoat ruffle of leaves or a heap of pebbles over a holder only serves to point it out, as well as adding another form, texture, or color, which may weaken the overall effect. Designers devise many original mechanics to meet demands and to assure that the plant parts are firmly implanted and will not lean, tilt, or push each other around the minute your back is turned.

## ❧❧❧ BEHOLD THESE HOLDERS

Basically there are two types of holders used in dried designing, the "frog" and the "foam." The frog type is most common and includes the *needlepoint*, which is heavy, rustproof, long-lasting, and easy to use. The *hairpin* is so irritating to use that if you have one, I suggest throwing it out. The *dragonfly* or *octopus*, made of strips of flexible plumber's lead, embraces each stem.

## ❧❧❧ FROG TECHNIQUES

Pinholders come in round, rectangular, interlocked and pin-cup types. Attach with a glob of room-temperature florist's clay. If, for some reason,

FIGURE 39

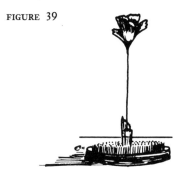

your clay will not cling (wet, cold, aged), run strips of nylon-reinforced tape over the frog in several directions.

Brace thin stems by putting a short piece of stem on each side; push a wire through horizontally, clip off ends. (Figure 39.)

For narrow leaves (daylily) cut a 1-inch piece from a surplus leaf, fold the piece over the bottom of the leaf to be used; the extra bulk holds.

FIGURE 40

Hard, tough stems are split vertically and wiggled onto needles.

## ❦❦❦ CLAY

The most common types are:

Florist's Flexible—green, reusable, reliable;

Tacky Tape (I call this White

Mule, it's so stubborn to remove. Try salad oil or cleaning fluid). Use with care as it will let go under strain, especially if warm.

## ❦❦❦ FOAM TECHNIQUES

Styrofoam is very lightweight and must be impaled on needle frog, or anchored in a puddle of melted wax, Hard-Set or linoleum paste, or purchased with adhesive base. If it is used on needles, place several layers of saran over them to prevent lodging of debris. Cut with sharp knife or jigsaw, sand with another piece of Styrofoam. Many paints and glues dissolve foam; use special products (Gard, Krylon).

Water-absorbent foams (nonspillable water) are commonly available as Oasis or Fil-Fast. Keep from crumbling and give support by wrapping in Pliofilm. Do not use aluminum foil—it's too harshly colored and textured. While this foam is a boon to the arranger of most flowers, fresh peonies and stocks seem to be allergic to its chemicals.

## ❦❦❦ HOLDERS FOR
## TALL CONTAINERS

Bringing the pinholder almost to the level of the container rim enables you to exercise greater control over your materials and reduces the need for extra long stems. Some practical ways of accomplishing this are:

"Loading" a container permanently by filling to within 2 to 3 inches of the top with sand, pea, road or bird gravel. Pour melted paraffin over this to about ½ inch above the gravel. Place a needle frog in the wax before it sets.

Or fill with sand, cover with a

FIGURE 41

thick pancake of floral clay.

Or fill with sand, make your design, and fix it by pouring wax over the sand.

## ❦❦❦ CLEAR CONTAINERS CONQUERED

Roll a "rope" of clay, take a turn around each stem, and press to container sides. Or use commercially available dragonfly.

FIGURE 42

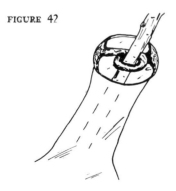

Make a sling of plumber's lead to hold a needle holder.

Slip a wide, tall leaf between confusing lines of material and the container's glass front; the leaf will seem to be an extension of the design.

Line the inside with crumpled Saran or foil to give interesting distortion.

FIGURE 43

## ❦❦❦ FRESH WITH DRIED

Wrap grapes or small potatoes in Saran, wire to stem, pierce, and poke stem of fresh bloom into the fruit.

Fill orchid or aqua tubes with water, affix with clay or tape.

Fill tiny toy balloons with water, add flower stem, mount with tape.

# SHAPING AND RESHAPING

Though nature carpenters an abundance of free-formed branches, twisted stems, and bark contortions through the effects of weather, crowding, or chemical damage, disciplined plant material is often needed to make a design. Purists should not fault manipulation as mutilation.

### 🌺🌺🌺 TO DISCIPLINE HEAVY BRANCHES, ROOTS:

Peel vines and branches by boiling a few minutes in a solution of 1 teaspoon soda to 1 quart of water. Use on wisteria, honeysuckle, barberry, elaeagnus, etc. Dried peeled vines can be resoaked overnight, starting in hot water, and reshaped, so don't be content with a single form.

Wrap any fresh material to be shaped with narrow fabric strips or hot towels. Apply towels several times, adjusting curves, and wire curved material. Let dry. If the materials are very brittle after drying,

snip the wire every 2 to 3 inches to avoid snapping the bough. Pussy willow, broom, cattails, apple, and quince respond to this.

To bend a solid plastic stem, place in very hot water, bend, and hold in ice water till curves are set.

Seed pods (okra, carob, etc.) can be soaked in hot water and shaped.

### 🌺🌺🌺 LEAF MANIPULATION

If you need a different shape or have a leaf with a torn edge, simply trim with scissors.

If liquid-treated leaves curl, soak in warm water two hours, then lightly massage. This works on leaves attached to stems (pear, crabapple) and on magnolia.

Coax package-dried cocklebur, castor bean, milkweed into contours by spraying with warm water until they no longer crackle; then gently shape.

# GROOMING

While most designers are careful to groom fresh plants, there seems to be a tendency to be more lax with drieds. Most clinging crumbs of granular medium will have been brushed away in removal and taping of plants. A second scrutiny should be given during the making of the design. It's the nature of viewers (detestable but true) to touch as soon as you say, "It's dried." A shower of granular dandruff at their

often indelicate touch is embarrassing, messy, and in competitive flower-show work will bring reductions under Condition and Distinction.

If you are nimble, pass roses, marigolds, larkspur, golden glow, etc., under a slow dribble of warm water, cupping in your hand and brushing gently with a soft brush. Dry quickly. Hemerocallis and daffodils are too moisture-susceptible to take this beauty bath. Try dampening the brush with water or Endust and quickly passing over petals.

Polish glossy leaves (magnolia, laurel, holly) with process liquid or olive oil or spray with Plant Shine.

## ❦❦❦ ADDING "STARCH" TO FLOWERS

Some flowers have such delicate tissue structure that a humid day can wilt them despite your best drying and storage procedures. I have little patience with "crutching," but sometimes extreme measures are needed to save a flower vitally needed to complete a design. To do this, attach threadlike wire to long straplike petals of daylilies and lilies by turning the flower over, laying wire on the petal back, dripping glue along the wire, laying a piece of magic tape over wire and glue, shaping, drying and trimming.

After all medium dust is removed, flowers and leaves can be given back-stiffening treatment by spraying with Krylon's Fixative #1306 or Plant Glaze (Bloomlife). Either protects from moisture, makes future cleaning easier, and brightens most colors.

If you want to preserve surface texture but give more body to your drieds, puff several coats of Tandy's Spray Glaze on the back only. This is especially successful on corsages of dried flowers.

## ❦❦❦ HOW LONG IS EVERLASTING?

Not all blooms stay sweet sixteen forever. How long a flower lasts depends more on its inborn textural composition than the process used. Generally, delicate types like tulips and hollyhocks have a shorter show life than marigolds, and marigolds a shorter life than strawflowers. However, careful storage in a dark dry place prolongs existence.

Use suit boxes (cover with Pliofilm to show off your work), add a drift of insecticide, a few mothballs to discourage mice, a few Dryox crystals, and label carefully.

Pressed or dried leaves are stacked by size and form in small plastic bags. But liquid-treated foliage must be tissue-wrapped to avoid skeletonizing.

Dried flowers, properly handled and cared for, will last several seasons, thereby earning the title "permanent," but therein lies an aesthetic danger—the almost irresistible compulsion to save everything with the hope of "needing it some day." Fortunately, lack of space is a counteracting factor for most of us. Another danger is becoming so attached to favorite pieces that you never re-examine them for creative new uses. If none presents itself, be hard-hearted enough to discard, thus making room for some new discovery that will inspire.

# TRANSPORTING

Generally you will have fewer mishaps if you build your creation at home and disassemble it to transport and remake at the site of the show, demonstration, or location. Sometimes this is not possible, so:

Keep a few loosely filled plastic sacks of sand; curve around container bases to keep from shifting.

If design is too tall to stand, lay flat on back, bracing with a few pillows.

If you've ever tried to reach into a cardboard box to retrieve a dried design, you know how easily blooms can be separated from stems. Cut down the front of the box, place the design in the now three-sided box, sandbag the base (or use blown-up balloons), tape up the front panel and drive off with confidence.

Always carry your design facing away from your body and in the direction you are going. You and the design will look better approaching (first impressions, and all that) and you'll be less apt to damage a "front-and-center" specimen.

Always carry a few spares of what is in your design (plus repair wire, glue, pliers, etc.), just in case a beheading occurs on the way. If this happens, clip stem off close to base of flower, push an insect pin and a glob of clay between the stem and flower base.

# 9 · Collector's Cupboard

The wealth of plant material that can be preserved is inexhaustible. Many useful species are not covered here, and this saves an untried area for your own exciting experiments. Look through the plants indexed below to find one of tissue structure similar to the one you want to try; note the recommended process. Or live dangerously: switch processes, and you may hit a winner. If you find a better way or a new one, do let me know.

Unless specified, allow the lowest number of days for silica gel, the middle number for mixtures with borax or Axion, the highest number for other granular mixtures.

### ❧❧❧ SEARCH FOR SOURCES

Each locality has its own natives awaiting your discovery and use in designs that will make others aware of nature's overlooked beauties. There are three major categories: yard and garden-grown plants; native, wild, and roadside; exotics, including tropicals, pot, and greenhouse plants.

Yards and gardens remain the best source of supply, since you as gardener-arranger can plant types that complement the decor of your home. Other sources include shops specializing in pods and supply houses that often furnish "wishbooks" on request, flower show "floratiques" (someone's discards may be just what you want), florist shops, both front- and backdoor. Friendly florists are now much more willing than in the past to order only three of some exotic leaf for you. And their trash barrels often brim with driable leftovers. The same can be said of flower shows. Haunt the backdoor at clean-up time. Exhibitors and committees alike are happy to donate blooms to continue life in dried form.

Fields, roadsides, even alleys, yield fascinating plants often unnaturally contorted by physical damage during the growing season—a delight for arrangers in search of free forms. A classic among arrangers is the story of the husband who, speeding along at 70 mph, is startled half out of his seat belt by his wife shrieking, "Stop, a lovely line!" He can't understand how, at such speed, she could have seen anything but a blur, and sometimes he's right. One such lovely line turned out to be a red-tagged highway marker that the long-suffering husband dubbed a horticultural find and ceremoniously named *Roadesia stakeosia*.

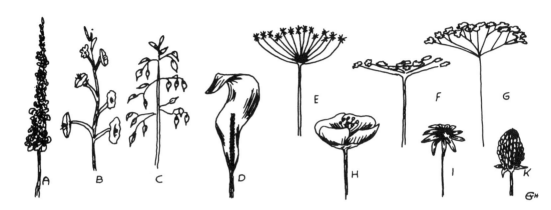

## TYPES OF INFLORESCENCE

*The plants you dry have many types of inflorescence or ways of blooming, as noted in the following listings.*

A SPIKE *Delphinium*
B RACEME *Lily-of-the-Valley*
 *Mallow*
C PANICLE *Seaoats, many grasses*
D SPATHE *Skunk-Cabbage*
E UMBEL *parsley*

F CYME *Viburnum, Snowball*
G CORYMB *Sweet William*
H SOLITARY *Poppy*
I COMPOSITE *Daisy*
K ROUNDED HEAD *Globe Amaranth*

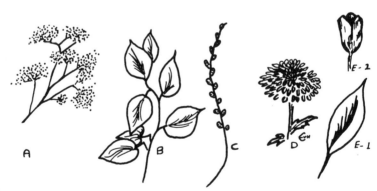

## TYPES OF MATERIALS

*The pattern of a design is established through the use of filler, line, and target types of materials.*

A FINE FILLER *Baby's Breath*
B MASS FILLER *Salal foliage*
C LINE, SPIKE, POINT *Pussy Willow*

D TARGET *Chrysanthemum*
E RELEASING INTEREST *1 Hosta Leaf*
 *2 Tulip Flower*

### Types of Design

*The most common contemporary types of design are:*

A LINE More space than solids.

B MASSED LINE Equal space and solids, definite focal area.

C MASS More solids than space.

D TRANSITION MODERN Bold designs and forms. Focal area still present, but lifting. Space beginning to be enclosed. Easy transition. Usually releasing boundary lines. Creative expression emerging. Somewhere between twentieth–century geometric and decorative arrangements and contemporary free expressions.

E FREE STYLE Free-formed branches and container. Nongeometric. Radiates from single or expected point. May have multiple interest areas (stamobile type).

F ABSTRACT and AVANT-GARDE Interest equated with design. Space enclosed or pierced or emphasized as focal area. Objects not chosen for identity but for design purpose. Objects often end with bold forms. May have multiple emergence points. Has impact, is bold, forceful, uncluttered.

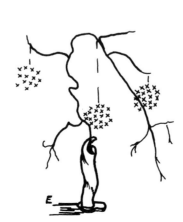

GUIDE TO DESIGNING

*Design is developed by using the elements (materials) according to the principles (ways of handling) to achieve beauty, simplicity, expression and harmony.*

The elements of design:
LINE sets the limits of a design. Line has character (weak, strong) and direction (diagonal, vertical, horizontal).
SPACE is emphasis on the "importance of nothing."
FORM is the 3-D (three-dimensional) shape of a design.
PATTERN is established by the silhouette (shadow) of solids and spaces.
COLOR is visual sensation.
TEXTURE is surface finish; it governs choice, sets the design character as masculine, feminine, refined, robust, etc.

The principles of design:
BALANCE is visual stability.
PROPORTION is relationship of areas to each other.
SCALE is the size of individual parts in relation to each other.
RHYTHM is the visual path created by repetition, gradation, line direction.
CONTRAST is emphasis on differences; adds "zing."
DOMINANCE is emphasis on similarities; brings unity, harmony, simplicity.

The elements of a flower arrangement:
Container · Base · Background · Mechanics · Accessories · Plant materials

# SELECTION OF PLANTS

ACHILLEA (Sneezewort) Perennial border herb. Clusters of small double white pompon flowers. Valuable individually in small or miniature arrangements and as filler in mass designs. Dry in granular mix in deep box to retain spray effect 2 to 4 days. (See also YARROW.)

AGAPANTHUS (Lily-of-the-Nile) Pot and border plant. Large starburst form tops sturdy natural stem. Air-dry. Use in large interpretive arrangements and for contrived forms.

AGAVE CACTUS. Includes century plant. Native, border, and pot plant. Swordlike coarse-textured blades. Available from suppliers of dried materials. Lay flat in closed shoebox 3 to 4 months. Dries to soft twilight colors. Leaves are ideal as strong structural modern lines. The three-valve seed pods are interesting additions when split.

ALLIUM Includes onion, garlic, chives, etc. Perennial border and edible bulbous herbs. Spherical clusters. White, yellow, pink, purple. To contort, partly pull up the plant, leaving just a few roots clinging to the soil; lay plant flat on the ground and it will develop fantastic curves. The curves can be retained when air- or granular-dried. An alternate method involves shaping when the buds are forming. Stems are pliable, especially in the heat of day. Bind with tape or wire into the wanted shape, tighten tape slightly each day for several days. Work gently, a little at a time. Let plant finish blooming and setting seed before cutting.

If the head on a nicely shaped stem is inadequate, remove and glue on a better one.

AMARANTH Border annuals. Love-Lies-Bleeding has long, odd, chenille-like drooping tassels. Maroon. Hang-dry. Use in massed line and contrived works. Globe Amaranth has round violet, red, white, and pink blooms. Pick when well matured at summer's end. Air-dry for small and miniature designs, corsages.

ANEMONE (Windflower) Perennial border herb. Cup-shaped. White, pink, purple, red. Numerous wild varieties. Obtain from florist for winter treatment. Remove stems, re-wire. Granular-treat 4 to 6 days. Good leaf subject also. Press flowers, leaves separately for 10 to 12 days. Store with drying medium as this is affected by humidity. Medium-size target form.

ANTHURIUM Tropical. White, pink, red. Has long brown spearlike seed pods. Both flower and foliage may be air-dried but they shrink excessively. May be resprayed to near-natural color. The glossy texture is lost during treatment with granular mix 8 to 10 days. The artificial product is so much like the natural with its patent-leather texture that it almost defies detection. Great silhouette value in modern, abstract designs. Air-dry the releasing target-form foliage.

APPLE See FRUIT TREES.

ARTICHOKE (Globe, French, Bur) Edible variety. Available dried from supply houses. Dries green, greeny-brown or tan; 2 to 4 inches in diameter. Parboil 10 minutes, rinse in cool water. Wedge shredded wax paper between scales during air drying to develop a full-blown flowerlike look. The large fluffy dried "flower" seed heads are available from florists and suppliers in many dyed colors. They greatly resemble CARDOON (which see), a cousin. Both fruit and seed heads are valuable as interest points in modern and abstract works.

ASPIDISTRA (Cast-Iron-Plant)  Pot plant. Flexible, glossy evergreen leaves. Available from florists. Freeze 4 hours, remove and hang-dry or simply air-dry by letting them stand in the design. May be resprayed green. Liquid treatment #1 also successful. Great in modern and abstract work as linear forms.

ASTER (China; also hardy and native species)  Varied colors. Glue before treating as they shatter easily. If shattered, use calyxes without the petals. Press singles separately or in short sprays 7 to 10 days. Preserve in granular mixes: singles of blue color 7 days, reds and purples 5 days; doubles of any color need 10 days. Valuable in mass, massed line design. Target form.

AUCUBA  Evergreen tender shrubs A. variegata is the Gold-Dust-Tree. Large leaves take liquid treatment #1 in 3 weeks. Darken to near-black. Hang upside down 3 days to distribute the solution and firm up the terminal leaves after treatment. Useful in interest areas of modern design and as mass filler.

AZALEA and RHODODENDRON  Native and yard shrubs. Hook-wire

florets separately and reassemble clusters after drying in granular mix 2 to 5 days. Store with drying crystals. Tape or glue to branches or group for large target forms. Valuable in mass, massed line, modern design interest areas. Foliage: treat glossy individual leaves in liquid #2 or rosettes and larger branches in liquid #1. Target or mass filler.

BABY'S-BREATH (Gypsophila paniculata)  Annual border plant. Hang-dry, stand upright or treat in granulated mix 3 days. Press 2 to 3 days. Use in pictures or as fine filler in mass designs, bouquets.

BACHELOR'S-BUTTON (Cornflower)  Annual, perennial border plant. Presses well in 7 to 10 days. Dry in granular mix 3 to 6 days. Useful in corsages, small designs, old-fashioned bouquets, or massed in bunches for interest areas in modern. The yellow-flowered Centaurea macrocephala has interesting round scaly pods.

BAMBOO  Many species. Press fern-like leaves 10 days. Use air-dried, cured stalks (purple, black joint and common yellow). Cut to various angles and lengths in free-style Oriental, modern and abstract designs.

BANANA  Many species, varieties. Tropical herb. Hang-dry leaves for surrealistic shapes; or lay on flat surface to air-dry. Good for modern, abstract arrangements. Treat the shiny leaves (lined with purple) of Banana-Shrub (Michelia fuscata) in liquid #1.

BAPTISTA (False-Indigo)  Native and border plant. Deeply cut foliage and blue, white, yellow lupinelike flowers in long terminal racemes.

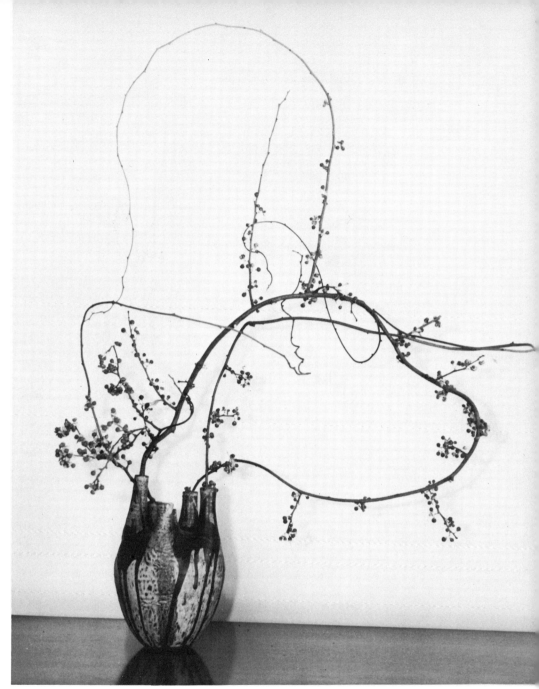

SWIRL OF BITTERSWEET  *To capture extensive spaces within a three-dimensional form, the designer uses no mechanics, but bends fresh stems to emerge from, and enter into, the several openings of the container. The stems are then air dried to set a simple pleasing pattern. There are satisfying similarities in the glaze of the ceramic container (by Esa Henderson) and the fruited lines of the bittersweet. These likenesses promote unity, while balancing the contrasts of straight lines and varied forms. Mrs. E. Walker, Illinois.*

Treat foliage with liquid #1, starting in warmed solution; after 6 days it turns dark blue. Dry flowers in granular mix 6 days. The short plump seed pods become gun-metal gray to blue-black when cut in the fall and hang-dried. Flowers press well in 6 to 7 days. Pressed leaves dry black in 6 to 7 days.

BARBERRY  Red or green foliages. Turns warm mellow brown after 10 days in liquid #1 if treated in the fall, and bright red if preserved in the spring. Remove thorns before processing. Will last several years with periodic rejuvenation with plant wax and oxblood shoe polish. Branches may be peeled to reveal the vivid yellow underlayer. Provides lines for modern linear designs. Attractive red, yellow, black berries last well when shellac-alcoholed. Use both foliage and berries in miniatures, corsages.

BEAD-TREE  Tropical tree or greenhouse subject. Air-dry the thin narrow 7-inch pods that coil when ripe and are filled with bright red lens-shaped seeds. Unusual linear material.

BEECH  American Beech. Yard tree *Fagus grandiflora* has lovely silky foliage, the European *F. atropunicea* (Purple Beech) has a copper variety. European *F. sylvatica* turns reddish brown in the fall. Treat when green or after the leaves lighten in autumn. All types process quickly in liquid #1, turning dark brown in 2 to 10 days. May be removed in 2 days while still green, though these leaves will eventually darken. Mass filler material.

BELLS-OF-IRELAND  Annual border plant. One of the favorites in dried designs. Remove foliage, glue green bells (bracts) to stems. Bells hold shape best if cut after the white flowers in the bell centers have bloomed; remove these with tweezers. Air-dry by hanging for ivory color, may stand in warm liquid #1 24 to 48 hours to maintain flexibility and color, then air-dry. Or use granular mix 4 days, which preserves the green, but the plants are brittle. If left in liquid #1 for 7 days, the result will be a pliable stem with bracts of a greeny-brown color. Remove at this point and hang upside down in a dark place. To attain a mellow brown color, use strong tea in the liquid #1 recipe in place of water, let process 2 weeks. Marvelous linear material, also valuable in corsages, wreaths, topiary work, contriveds when bracts are wired and used individually.

BITTERSWEET  Yard vine. Highly prized for colorful yellow fruits with red appendages. Available commercially or cut from home gardens. Observe conservation of native plants in some states. Spray with fixative for several seasons of beauty. Lovely linear curves.

BOXWOOD  Evergreen yard shrubs, trees. Process small leaves in liquid #1 for 4 days or submerge in liquid #2 for 4 days for golden hue. Or stand to dry in small amount of water until moisture in container evaporates. Filler material.

BROCCOLI  Edible garden plant. Cut heads from thick heavy stems and process 7 to 14 days in granular mix. Use in contrived forms or bunched for target material. Retains deep green but may be sprayed. Leaves air-dry to warm tan with delicate mauve tints. Cabbage and cauliflower foliage can be handled this way. See also KALE.

BULRUSH AND RUSHES Roadside plants. Thought to be named for the top spike used to prod cattle into moving faster. Several species. Stand, hang or press. May be curved fresh or may be soaked and reshaped when once dried. Great linear forms.

BURDOCK (Cocklebur) Biennial, perennial roadside plant. The large leaves may be package-wrapped or air-dried. They may be dampened and reshaped once they have been dried, but care must be taken not to tear them. The burs may be gathered when immaturely green or mature dark brown. They cling tightly together and are very handy in making contrived forms, novelties, wreaths, figures, topiary trees. No special processing needed.

CACTUS Many species. Native, pot plants. Very interesting forms, good for interpretive works. See OPUNTIA (cholla), AGAVE, DESERTSPOONFLOWER and also saguaro "boots" (page 78). Flowers of many species dry exquisitely when processed in granular mix 2 to 8 days, depending upon petal substance. Some pads may be skeletonized.

CALLA Border or pot plant. White, yellow. Stuff flower with wax paper and hang dry, though there will be much shrinkage. Better to use silica gel 7 to 8 days. Process foliage by granular method, hanging or pressing. Stunning in interpretives, Oriental, and contemporary designs.

CAMELLIA Evergreen tree, shrub. White, pink, red target-type flowers in singles, doubles. Glossy green foliage is treated in liquid #1 or #2 or granular mix. Granular-treat flowers 2 to 7 days, depending on type. Don't touch the petals as this causes dark bruises. May also be waxed. Foliage and flowers pleasing in mass, massed line, modern interpretations.

CANNA Border and pot plant. Foliage bronze, green. Treat with liquid #1 or #2 for 5 to 7 days. Or pick leaves after frost for fine brown color. Or process in granular mix 4 to 6 days—use both flat and rolled center leaves, make some loops and folds to add depth to designs; or package press. Ideal in large contemporary works.

CARDOON (Cardone) Tropical. The large fluffy dried "flower" pompons closely resemble those of their relative, the artichoke, and are available in many dyed colors from suppliers and florists.

CARNATION (Dianthus, Pinks) Border perennials. Press singles 5 to 7 days or dry in granular mix 3 to 4 days. Increase the length of time for drying the larger florist types. Twist "gone" petals from large types and use the bell-shaped calyxes in small designs, contrived forms, and corsages.

CASTOR BEAN Border plant. Many types. The large leaves may be frozen 48 hours, then hung upside down to achieve long, twisting tubes excellent for modern and avantgarde work. The leaves may also be flat-dried and then cut to various shapes (star, etc.). Or strip away all tissue, leaving only the veins to dry at the tip of the stem. The large stalks may be handled the same as bamboo. The seed pods make intriguing clusters for interest areas in many types of arrangements. Poisonous.

CATTAIL  Perennial roadside plant. Stately and decorative spikes of odd brown "flowers." Brown or greenish, depending on the gathering season. May be sprayed, jeweled, topped with puffballs, etc. Spray with clear plastic fixative to check "exploding." The pencil-slim size is commercially available; or gather from the roadside at whatever size and color desired. If green, place in liquid #1 for 3 days. A bunch of immature "cats" were accidentally left in an unshaded car trunk during several hot summer days and they twisted into fantastic shapes. The hollow stems are fine extenders. The reedlike foliage may be hang-dried or pressed and used in designs or woven into mats for bases or dining table. All parts are indispensable to the arranger.

CECROPIA  Tropical tree. When dried, the large, lobed leaves are a lovely soft gray with brownish-red veining on the back and front. Dried leaves can be soaked and reshaped. They can be used as an open "hand" or closed "fist" form for either target or linear positions in newer concept designing. The fresh leaves may also be treated with liquid #1.

CELOSIA. (Cock's-comb) Annual border plant. *C. cristata* (crested) has dense, plushlike shapes sometimes grotesquely flattened, or ruffled like a cocks-comb. *C. plumosa* (plumed) has feathery delicate-appearing heads. Colors are red, gold, pink, white, orange. Cut the plumed type as soon as color is fully developed and before seeds begin to drop to prevent "molting" and a moth-eaten effect. Gather crested type before seeds set. Remove foliage. Air-dry both crested and plumed after standing them in hot liquid #1 for 24 hours in a dark place. The bit of solution absorbed helps retain color and reduces shedding. The crested may also be fully treated with liquid #1 7 to 9 days. Press small pieces 7 days. The plumed type is useful in mass or linear work, the crested makes artistic additions to interpretive and new concept arrangements.

CHINESE LANTERN (Winter-Cherry) Border perennial. Grown for flaming orange-red balloonlike husks which may be split and turned back, or slashed along veins for odd curling effects. If picked green, they will remain so when hang-dried. Balloons may be removed from the natural stalks and individually wired for unusual effects. If the pods are too far apart to suit your purpose, fasten extra ones on with floral tape. Makes a colorful addition of target or linear form.

CHIVES  Perennial garden herb. Small quarter-sized globular lavender flowers. Dry in granular mix 3 days. Use as target form in small designs, or bunch together for larger ones.

CHRYSANTHEMUMS  Annual, perennial border plants. Extensive color range but yellow and pink dry best. Success with chrysanthemums is sporadic, as the colors are often fugitive and petals fall. Experiment with your available varieties. Some will surprise you by drying beautifully. Small pompons can be hang-dried with slight shrinkage and resprayed their former color. Glue petals to

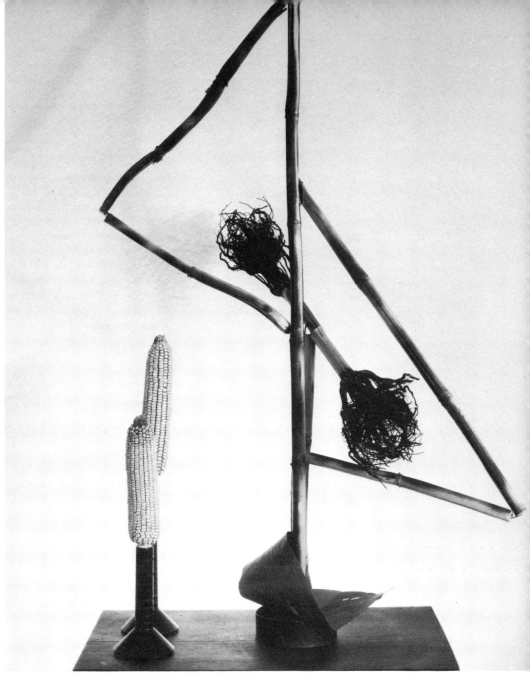

FROM THESE ROOTS  *No container other than a pinholder is used but the strategically placed leaf gives the appearance of a free-formed supportive shape. Abstract in construction, the various plant parts are used as pure form, color, and line; awareness of these comes first, and only later recognition of origin. The design illustrates that every part, from root to fruit, of a common plant is beautiful and, through strong diagonals denoting motion and power, the designer expresses her personal feeling of the importance of corn. Mrs. J. Kestel, Iowa.*                                                    [*Walden Photos, Inc.*]

calyx before drying 7 to 15 days in granular mix. Singles make excellent pressed flowers. Press petals of larger mums separately 7 to 21 days. Variable results.

CLEMATIS Woody climbing vine. Native and garden plant. White, pinks, reds, blues, purples. Two main types: (1) large-flowered (*C. jackmani*, etc.) and (2) small-flowering (Virgin's Bower). To preserve large flowering types, glue sepals to calyx, granular-treat 4 to 5 days. Silica gel 2 to 3. May be pressed 10 days. Beautiful, ethereal target flowers for many design types. Process small flowers in spray on natural stems 3 to 5 days. Submerge seed pods in liquid #2 solution 24 hours or stand upright to dry.

COCKLEBUR See BURDOCK.

COCK'S-COMB See CELOSIA.

CONES In variety. Used in innumerable ways in designs, wreaths, topiary, corsages, etc. May be gathered at various times during the season to obtain a variety of sizes and colors.

CORN Various ornamental and edible types differing in size, form, color. Gather ears when mature, pull back the husks, air-dry. Air-dry the tassels of garden and field varieties either by hanging or standing. Husks and leaves ideal when air-dried or pressed 5 to 6 days. See ideas in Chapter 6 on contriveds for making novelty decorations. Field cornhusks have more substance for making "flowers."

STRAWBERRY ORNAMENTAL CORN: Delightfully tiny mahogany-red ears (1 to 2 inches long, 1½ inches thick) are fascinating additions to many compositions when glued to extender stems. Use nubbins in corsages.

RAINBOW or INDIAN CORN: Has endless combinations of red, orange, yellow, blue, and purple kernels on normal-sized ears. Valuable for harvest themes, swags and individual kernels for mosaics or pictures. Corn foliage is air-dried to give designs a tropical look. The stalks provide strong, straight, structural lines in new concept interpretations. May be left natural gold, or sprayed, or painted with stripes.

CROTON Tropical shrub, pot plant, or from florist. Striking color veinings on long narrow leaves. Liquid process #1 for 10 to 15 days; colors will dim. Hues hold better if placed in 1 inch of water and left in dark place until water is evaporated. Or granular-treat for 8 to 15 days, depending upon substance. Ideal for strong modern designs.

CYPRESS (Bald) Deciduous native. Produces the unusual decorative wood forms known as "cypress knees" beloved of designers as accessories. The knees are formed to bring air to the roots when the swamp habitat floods. Saw off interestingly shaped chunks, wax to highlight smooth brown surface. Available from florists and suppliers.

DAFFODIL *Narcissus* is the botanical name. Jonquil is but one family member. Yellows and oranges, white. Florets of jonquils, tazettas, and other types with more than one flower to a stem are wired, dried individually, and reassembled. Use granular mixes (silica gel recommended) with varying number of days for doubles, cluster-type florets, and cup varieties. Short-cup types with red or orange predominating in the cup retain brighter color with little shrinking. Store with Dryox and use in humidity-free atmosphere. Small types press satisfactorily in 7 to 8 days. Excellent for spring interpretive designing. To preserve the straplike foliage, lay between unweighted newspapers, or hang for twisted forms.

DAHLIA  Border tuber. Wide color range. Hook-wire. Experiment with your available varieties. Cactus types do not hold their curved margins, and pompons tend to lose their quilled petals unless glued. Seed dahlias in singles, anemone types, and miniatures are successful when held 5 to 6 days in granular mix. Larger types take 10 days. Support each layer of petals on larger petals. Target form.

DAISY  Native and cultivated border plant. African, Gerbera (Transvaal Daisy), Cape Marigold, Gloriosa, Michaelmas, Black- and Brown eyed Susan, Shasta and other daisylike flowers, *Rudbeckia*, etc., take similar treatment. Glue petals at center. Let glue dry thoroughly. Hook-wire. Granular-treat for 3 days. Common Meadow Daisy and Gerbera take 5 days. Press 5 to 7 days.

DAYLILY (*Hemerocallis*)  Border perennial. Yellow, orange, greens. A very exotic dried flower, but a temperamental one that needs shaping during the final drying process and protective storage. Display in humidity-low atmosphere to prevent drooping. Dry in granular mix 5 to 10 days, testing often. Process buds

also. Use as target forms in modern abstract designs. The seed pods are valuable additions to your collection and may be sprayed, glittered, and used in contrived forms, corsages.

DELPHINIUM and LARKSPUR  Annual, perennial border plants. Blues to purples, whites, pinks. One of the most satisfactory and valuable for spike form, and ideal in various types of design. Dries easily in granular mix 5 to 6 days. Individually wired florets require only 2 to 3 days. Presses well in 5 days. May be hang-dried, but loses character through tissue shrinkage.

DEVIL'S-CLAW  See  UNICORN PLANT.

DESERT SPOONFLOWER  Rare native desert plant. Do not pick from roadside; acquire from supplier or home garden and display only with note stating source. So popular that, fearing extinction, conservationists urge protective laws and home culture. Leaves are long, stiff, slender except at the base, which is broad, ivory-colored, and spoon shaped where leaves overlap; when cleaned and polished, they are placed upside down in designs and clearly suggest their common name. Fine in modern, abstract, avant-garde works.

DOGWOOD  Native and cultivated tree, shrub. If gathering from roadside, consult conservation list as this is protected in many states. Pink, white. Dry florets individually in granular mix 4 to 6 days. Reassemble, copying natural formation. Foliage may be treated with liquid #1 or pressed. Line or filler in various designs. Air-dry red branches of Red-Osier Dogwood.

Dusty miller  A common name given several plants characterized by white woolly foliage. Gather in September. Usually air-dried upside down, but extra nice if done in granular mix 5 to 7 days. Excellent for special color harmonies and to soften transition between intense color companions.

Echinops  See Thistle.

Elaeagnus  Several species. Evergreen and deciduous trees. Russian Olive is common name for *E. angustifolia*. Treat with liquid #1 for 6 weeks. Leaves remain silvery underneath and turn deep golden on surface. Treat other species in same manner. Useful as filler, for linear forms and special color harmonies. Foliage is scaled fine enough for miniatures.

Eucalyptus  (Blue-Gum Tree) Spiral (Dollar) eucalyptus is commercially available and is grown in warm climates. Pungently fragrant, long, arching boughs of gray-green round leaves closely placed. Air-dry or process in warm liquid #1. The length of time since the branch was cut affects the color and absorption speed. 1 week for freshly shipped, 2 to 3 weeks for older shipments. The color is capricious, sometimes remaining a natural soft gray-green or pinkish-gray or becoming a rich mahogany brown. Wire individual leaves for corsages, small designs, topiary, wreaths. Use full branches for wedding decorations and linear design forms. Treat berries with shellac-alcohol; they remain green and serve for contrived forms, corsages.

Everlastings, immortelles  A

name given several species with flowers of papery quality. This includes Cupid's Dart, Statice, Sea-Lavender, Globe Amaranth, Baby's-Breath, Pearly Everlastings and Strawflowers. Gather just before maturity and hang-dry or press 3 to 5 days. The "tinies" available from florists are called starflowers and are excellent (as are the above) in corsages, miniatures, or grouped as target forms or in contriveds.

Fern  Various species. Native, border and pot plant. Using an artist's wide brush, apply olive oil to both sides. Press under weights 3 weeks. Press Royal Fern 3 months. Ferns can also be treated in granular mix 5 to 9 days. Fronds may be bleached before processing. Duck-foot Fern (Gansoku *Matteuccia*) is tall, vigorous, with broad, palmlike fronds. Stand dry for strong linear material.

Feverfew  Perennial border plant. White. Singles, doubles. Too bad all chrysanthemums are not as easy as this old-time favorite. The tiny button blooms may be removed from the main branch, wired, and used individually in miniatures, or the entire branch buried in a deep box in granular mix 4 to 5 days. Warmth helps to retain whiteness. Fine filler.

Forsythia  Cascading yard shrub. Tape or wire curves to box bottom. Cover with granular mix 5 to 6 days. Excellent pressed 5 days. Liquid #1 turns foliaged branches light brown. The wealth of brilliant yellow flowers on leafless branches makes superb additions to mass, crescent, Hogarth curves and interpretive-of-spring arrangements.

Fruit trees  Cultivated and roadside small trees. Processed and dormant branches elegant in many design categories especially interpretive and free style.

CRABAPPLE: Process foliaged branches in liquid #1 in early fall. Flowering branches in granular mix 5 to 7 days. Also applies to other apples.

WEEPING CRABAPPLE: Process fruit semipermanently in silica gel 3 weeks.

PEACH: Cut blossoming sprays in bud, granular-treat 5 to 7 days. Liquid #1 for foliaged branches.

PLUM: Place flowering sprays, cut in bud, in granular mix 5 to 7 days. Leaves are capricious in liquid #1. Add red food coloring to process Flowering Plum for glossy red color.

PEAR: Difficult to prevent petal drop from flowering branches. Foliage excellent; turns almost black after treating in liquid #1 for 3 to 4 days. Unusual for contemporary work. Linear and fine filler.

FUNGI (Including mushrooms, shelf and bracket fungi, etc.) Air-dry with support of shredded paper to prevent sagging if individual structure indicates that this may happen. Small types can be wired to form flowerlike rosettes; use in wreaths, corsages, etc. Fascinating forms and textures of larger types make superb additions to advanced undertakings. Distorted mangrove roots have a similarity of form.

GARLIC See ALLIUM.

GERANIUM Perennial border or pot herb. Wide color range which holds true when pressed 5 to 7 days. Granular-dry 5 to 6 days. Useful in mass and traditional designs and as

focal areas in modern and interpretive works.

GLADIOLUS Tender cormous border plant. Wide color range, though whites, pinks, and orange dry best. The miniature varieties are most successful. All take 10 days to press, 8 to 10 in granular mix. Include tips. Dry florets separately, reassemble onto heavy wire in natural position. Foliage may be treated in liquid #1, or hang-dried to get twists. Respray. Use in mass, massed-line, modern designs. Fully open florets excellent in interest areas as target forms.

GLOBE AMARANTH See AMARANTH.

GLOBE THISTLE See THISTLE.

GOATSBEARD, PUFFBALL See SALSIFY.

GOLDEN GLOW Perennial border plant. Yellow. Granular mix 5 to 7 days, or press 5 to 6 days. Since the form is similar, Golden Glow may be red-sprayed to simulate carnations. Medium target form useful in many types.

GOLDENROD Many species. Roadside perennial. Inflorescence varies from clusters of tiny flowers to feathery panicles. For best results gather when about three-quarters of the florets have opened. Air-dry by hanging upside down or press small pieces 5 to 6 days. Most noteworthy as filler in mass designs, though should be handled more creatively. Also used in corsages, miniatures.

GOURDS Many species, varieties. Properly cured gourds have been known to last 100 years. Designs may be burned on, indented, or carved

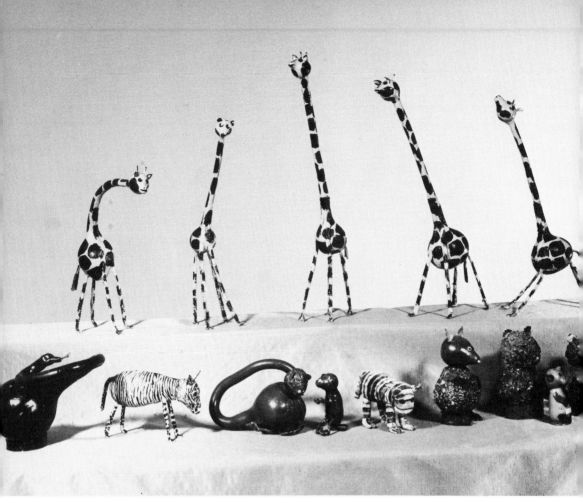

ANIMAL FARM *A little paint, a lot of imagination, turn garden gourds into a botanical zoo worthy of Noah's attention. Dipper and "alley-oop" gourds are trellis grown, hung down to develop long straight handles. If left on the ground, they may contort naturally, or they may be taped or tied into desired positions. Eyes, ears, bills, tongues, feet, and bases are shaped from cardboard and painted. Chenille-wire legs give a realistic look. Humorous positions are often possible with a little preplanning. Mrs. C. Sparkman, North Carolina.* ["Doc" Johnson Studios]

during the growing season. Shapes may be altered by growing in flasks or molds or by taping. Pick when stem turns brown and before frost. Prick ends of harvested gourds with a long needle or ice pick to speed interior drying. Hang in open-mesh potato bags 3 to 6 months. Gourds should not be used for craft work until the seeds rattle inside. Don't be disturbed by softening and draining liquids. It's at this stage that many are discarded because people think they are rotting. Check regularly, wiping away any moisture if you want to prevent mosaic patterns. When gourds have dried, coat with clear shellac, or spray-paint as desired. Useful as containers, accessories or unique forms in the bodies of many types of design. Especially fine in harvest and Thanksgiving interpretations. Grotesque shapes good for abstract designing. See also LUFFA.

GRASSES AND GRAINS Cereal, ornamental, roadside. Generally hang-dry in small bunches as most orchard and common grasses fluff up during the drying process. To curve, stand in large-necked receptacles. Press 5 to 9 days. May stand in jars of dye, which will be partly absorbed before drying. Treatment with liquid #1 or #2 for 2 weeks keeps grasses, grains flexible. Many take well to crystallizing. Tips useful in corsages and as stamens in contriveds. May be bleached or sprayed. Fine filler.

GUM See SWEET GUM.

HELICONIA Greenhouse tropical. Hang-dry. The boat-shaped sheaths become exotic, sinister-appearing additions to avant-garde and interpretive creations.

HENBANE Roadside herb. Air-dry. Long arching spikes of bell-shaped seed pods. Stalks often dry naturally curved. Spray or flock. Liquid treatment #1 turns green henbane brown-yellow and leaves it supple. Ideal for Christmas interpretives, crescents, Hogarth curves (S curves) and other vertical and curvilinear works. Or wire individual bells for use in corsages, wreaths, etc.

HOLLY Shrub or tree. Liquid treatment # 1 takes only 3 days. Air-dry for olive-green color. Berry life will be semipermanent if dipped into alcohol-shellac. See Semipermanent Processing, page 92.

HOLLYHOCK Biennial, perennial border plant. White, pink, yellow, red, doubles and singles. Gather when color begins to show in buds; hang-dry. The tissuelike quality contributes an ethereal touch to many types of design. Dry buds to substitute as rosebuds. Granular mix 5 to 6 days, or silica gel #2. Sear ends of stems before drying. Press 5 days. Needs tender loving care to prevent damage. Superb as target and linear forms.

HONESTY (Lunaria) Also known as Money-plant or Satin-Pod. Annual, perennial border plant. Quarter-sized silver pods. When the pods are mature, hang-dry until tan, rub off outer covering to reveal the transluscent disks. No further treatment needed but may be sprayed, dyed, rewired to individual pieces, or glued into pictures, corsages, collages, or contriveds.

HOSTA (Funkia, Plantain-Lily) Border perennials. Many species. Large, conspicuously ribbed and quilted leaves, some margined and splotched with white, green and blue-green. See special processes for speed-heat drying, or package wrap. Mass filler or target forms.

HYACINTH (Dutch) Border bulb. The spikes of highly fragrant florets come in many colors. Individual florets may be granular-dried 5 days, reassembled to spike form. I accidentally discovered that individual fresh florets strung lei-fashion air-dry with little shrinkage; the white turns ivory, but it can be resprayed. Linear material, cascade effects, contriveds, corsages, or small designs.

HYACINTH BEAN: Collect the interesting purple or green pods in October. Air-dry.

HYDRANGEA Deciduous yard shrub and pot plant. Large clusters of showy white, green, pink, blue. Gather PeeGee in early fall. Pink Oakleaf in May, June. *H. grandiflora* (Hills of Snow) may be air-dried upside down in either its early white or more mature green stage, or granular-treated 3 to 5 days. Treat *H. hortensis* (pink or blue florist type) in granular mix 3 to 5 days. Clusters can also be treated with liquid #1 6 to 10 days. Results will be flexible and a soft fawn brown. Petals and florets press in 5 days. Dried clusters can be wired or attached to curving natural branches of other plants for use in large modern designs. Use tiny individual flowers in miniature or small designs, corsages. Large clusters sprayed vivid colors form target shapes in avantgarde creations.

IRIS None of my large bearded iris has proved truly successful. Beardless Siberian, Spuria, Bulbous Dutch, Reticulata, Vesper and Crested are more successful in granular mix 5 to 7 days, silica gel 3 to 5 days. Foliage may be pressed 7 to 10 days, or treated with liquid #1 for 12 days or hang-dried for twisted effects. May also be granular-dried 6 days. Try a few with loops and curls and dry in that position. *I. foetidissima* is scarlet-fruited in three-segmented pods; all other types have interesting seed pods to use natural or sprayed or in contrived forms, making iris a versatile plant. There used to be a saying regarding butcher shops that "they used everything but the pig's squeal." Iris is rather like that, as I have seen even the fleshy rhizomatous roots used as target forms in mod interpretations.

IVY All species and varieties preserve nicely when subjected to leaf immersion with liquid #2 treatment. Stitch-wire and reassemble after drying. The prominent nodes and tendrils of Grape Ivy (without foliage) make it interesting linear material; shape while still fresh and wire until dried. All types excellent for cascading, Hogarth curves, mass designs, corsages, wreaths, etc.

JACARANDA Tropical American tree, shrub. Cut pods in half lengthwise so exquisite interior shows in corsages, etc. Both the pods and fernlike foliage available from pod shops.

JERUSALEM OAK Tuber-bearing sunflower. Annual. Its long contorted stems are a favorite with modern designers. Air-dry.

JUNIPER Evergreen shrub. Pound ends, stand in liquid #1 for 10 days. Many design uses. Alcohol-shellac dip for the blue berries.

KALANCHOE (*K. beharensis*) Perennial pot and greenhouse herb. The large, velvety leaves air-dry, forming grotesquely curled shapes, but retain the plush look. Mellow brown with orangy tints. Modern, avant-garde, exotic target forms.

KALE Flowering or ornamental. Pot or garden plant. White to cream, pink, orchid, green crinkly foliage. The cabbage-sized heads, made up of the curled fluted leaf edges, silica-gel-dry in 7 days. Stunning in many modern, avant-garde plans.

KELP   Seaweed. Available at some suppliers or gather from the beach. Dry in sun and open air to avoid smell. Can be made soft, pliable (though odorous) by soaking in warm water and reshaping over and over. If used with fresh material, mount on sticks above water to avoid softening. Use a few upside down so the roots simulate some dark weird flower. Splendid for free-style, linear, and interpretives.

LARKSPUR   See DELPHINIUM.

LAUREL   Many plants called laurel really belong to other genera than the true Sweet Bay. Cherry-Laurel is *Prunus laurocerasus;* Trailing Arbutus, called Ground-Laurel is *Epigaea repens.* All absorb liquid #1 in 4 days to several weeks. Sweet Bay's dark glossy 4-inch leaves turn brown in liquid #1 after 10 days. Treat Ground-Laurel in liquid #2, stitch-wire, and reconstruct vine.

LICHENS   Similar to fungi, some are highly colored. Bake at 250 degrees F. until dry to destroy spores. Wire into rosette forms or glue to ends of interestingly shaped branches. Use in designs, corsages, collages, wreaths.

LILAC   (Syringa)   Hardy yard shrub. A good-natured subject in all colors when granular-dried 4 to 6 days. Retains much fragrance, but shrinks if hang-dried several weeks. White color "creams" in most processes; try applying slow heat and add more salt to the granular mix. Pick before fully opened. You can press for 5 days, but poor for press-

ing as it often browns or fails to hold true color. The trusses of small flowers are charming both in mass and massed-line designs and deserve more than the usual mediocre bunching. Use small clusters in tiny arrangements. The interesting seed clusters are useful individually or bunched; color may be altered.

LILY   Bulb. Many species and varieties. Experiment with those you have, as results are variable. The Orange Cup (*L. philadelphicum*) silica-gel treated 6 to 16 days is usable for several seasons. Trumpet or funnel types (Madonna) and bowl types (Gold Band) are tricky to store. Upright forms (*L. umbellatum* and its many Golden Chalice hybrids) are variable. The smaller varieties and hybrids of the reflex forms (*L. martagon* and Fiesta hybrids) and the bowl hybrids (Empress) are most successfully dried 5 to 7 days in silica gel. Rewire. Very useful as target forms. *L. umbellatum* has interesting stalks that stay green with liquid #1 treatment and *L. philippinense* has long exotic pods clustered at the top of wiry stems, fine for modern structures.

LILY-OF-THE-VALLEY   Low perennial herb. Do flower spike in granular mix 3 days, or press for 5 days, but it is very poor presser as it browns. Fragrance lingers long after processing. The small graceful spike of white blossoms is appropriate in small designs, corsages. Liquid #2 treatment turns the wide foliage black-green. Or use the speed-heat process. Releasing target form.

LOCUST   Yard tree. Air-dry the flattened, curving, glossy brown-to-nearly-black pods for use in many types of contemporary designs.

LOTUS  Pods available from florist and suppliers. Bowl-shaped pods have top dotted with round holes. The smaller ones are noteworthy as releasing target forms, the full-sized serve in interest areas of newer concept designs. Mount on extender stems for greater handling ease.

LOVE APPLES  Small greenhouse shrub. Small hard shiny orange fruits popular in dried-flower arrangements. Florists' supply.

LOVE-LIES-BLEEDING  See AMARANTH.

LUFFA (Dishcloth Gourd)  Air-dry or purchase from suppliers. Leave hard skin on or peel off for textural changes. Unusual cucumber-shaped, sometimes contorted, fibrous plant form to use as accessory or within the body of contemporary designs. Can be cut into cross sections and wired into unusual flowers.

LUNARIA  See HONESTY.

LYTHRUM (Loosestrife)  Tall, hardy, border perennial. Rose to purple. Press short 3- to 4-inch spike ends 7 days, or bury entire spike in granular mix 6 to 8 days. Useful in vertical line designs and mass designs as fine filler.

MAGNOLIA  Evergreen yard tree, shrub. The earlier in the season, the faster branches absorb and the darker the color. Vary by doing some all summer. Several days standing in liquid #1 gives a greenish mottled effect; allow 3 weeks for full absorption and a mellow brown color. In-

dividual leaves can be submerged in liquid #2. A few small leaves should also be processed for use in corsages and small designs. Branches and leaves are indispensable in all design types, for craft items, and they last up to three years without change in character. May be skeletonized. Boiling in soapy water turns them white. Air-dried, the leaves turn a silver green. All types can be heavily enamel-painted for special effects: Magnolia buds may be air-dried; the flowers dry beige even in silica gel. Cut from curving branches before they open and handle carefully as they bruise easily. Glue petals after thoroughly dry. Magnolia has interesting seed pods of large size; spray these with plastic fixative. Releasing target form.

MANZANITA  Evergreen shrubs. Large, many-crooked branches, unique linear shapes for free styling. Red when freshly dried and protected, grays if weathered.

MAPLE  Red, Ash-leafed, Japanese, Amur. Yard trees. Experiment with liquid #1 on species available to you. Submerge individual leaves and clusters in liquid #2, reassemble to branches. The delicate lobed branches of Japanese and Amur can be carefully curved and dried in granular mix 9 days; or package-press, or air-dry. Fine filler and line material.

MARE'S TAIL  Aquatic and bog herb. Often available from suppliers. Contorted line similar to Jerusalem Oak; grows about 2 feet tall. New-concept designs.

MARIGOLD  Annual border plant. Yellow and orange. Excellent for

THE MODERN LOOK  *A bold, massed-line design of limited materials is de-veloped by employing space as an important element within this 40-inch design. A heavy philodendron root and a dried mullein rosette constitute an unusual expression with double paralleled focal areas, one .of space, one of mullein, in an effective balance. Mrs. A. Mullins, Florida.*

pressing. Press singles 10 days, 14 for doubles. Granular-treat large doubles 10 to 14 days, singles 7. Pick before calyx splits, hook-wire. May also be hang-dried, but shrinkage is severe. Since marigolds have the same form as carnations, you can pass them off as such by spraying red. Target or filler.

MILKWEED Roadside perennial. Green-to-purple flower clusters lose color when granular-dried (5 to 8 days), but the interesting fist-sized starry form is usable anyway; may be spray-painted. May be air-dried, but drastic shrinkage results. Press flowers and leaves 7 days. Immerse leaves in liquid 8 days for dark green. The main interest for the designer is the petal-shaped seed pod, which is used in many types of arrangements and craft work. Pods may be picked green when still complete, or later when fully mature and burst to reveal the ivory interior contrasting with the woolly gray exterior. Remove silk. No further attention needed. Mount on extender stems, glue to contorted branches, or use as is.

MITSUMATA (*Edgeworthia papyrifera*, Paperbush) The branches have the fascinating habit of branching three twigs from each joint. Smooth white texture. Excellent linear form. Use in Oriental-influenced and newer concept works. Available from suppliers.

MOCKORANGE Deciduous yard shrub. White. Press individual flowers or short sprays 5 days. Granular-treat 3 to 5 days. Excellent. Fine filler or linear material. The soft-centered stems serve well as natural stem extenders for elevating dried flowers.

MONKEY-PUZZLE Tree. Stiff, sharp-pointed leaves closely attached and placed on curved and twisted branches. Dark brown when air-dried. Excellent linear material. Color may be altered. Startling in contemporary works.

MONSTERA See PHILODENDRON.

MULLEIN Hardy biennial roadside herb. Dense woolly gray rosettes of foliage air-dry when supported on pinholder with stuffing of shredded paper between the leaves (14 days). Gently massage the leaves daily as long as limp to retard twisting, unless this condition is desired. The whole velvety rosette or individual leaves may be pressed 10 to 18 days. The dried stalks have a warty surface and grow to over 6 feet. Striking linears in modern, abstract, and avant-garde designs especially when they fasciate naturally or are chemically contorted by weedkillers. Stalks are dark brown when air-dried on the plant to maturity, but may be gathered when green, which lightens to grayed green. Easily sprayed to alter color.

NEW ZEALAND FLAX Perennial herb. Long strap leaves, sharp black-satin seed pods. Needs no further treatment. Linear.

NUTS (all kinds) Dry in shallow layers. Spray with insecticide to cut down on boarders. May be sprayed, sparkled, waxed, etc. See Contrived What-Is-Its, Chapter 6. It may solve flower-show classification problems to know that walnuts, acorns, chestnuts, pecans, filberts, Brazil nuts are

DESERT ABSTRACT  *This design, built on two qualities of visual motion—repetition and line direction—has broken the surrounding space into exciting but unified patterns. The dominant design line is vertical, in strong contrast to the impudent repetitions that force the eye to sweep rhythmically from side to side in a balanced-counterbalanced visual path. Despite the use of three pieces on the table surface, no base is needed since the desert spoonflower and two sections of cholla (opuntia) overlap to create a continuous effect. Kathryn Holley Seibel, Ohio.*  [*W. Seibel photo*]

true nuts, while peanuts, coconuts, almonds (which are kernels of a peachlike fruit) are not true nuts. All types may be lightened by soaking in pure laundry bleach.

OAK Yard and native tree. In July, pick branches just as the green acorns are forming, air-dry. Foliage is commercially preserved and available from florists in brilliant orange-yellow combinations for corsages, wreaths, or stem-extended; fine filler in designs. Process Pin Oak in liquid #1 for warm browns. Or completely immerse single and clustered leaves and reassemble for fine filler. Oak acorns and galls may be group-wired for interest areas and in wreaths.

OKRA Annual herb. Long, ribbed pods are cut before frost, air-dried. Split or leave intact for use in many types of design, including mobiles. May be wired to longer wires or curved branches of other plants to facilitate handling in contemporary works.

OPUNTIA (*O. cylindrica*, Cholla or Desert Lacewood) Roadside desert cactus. Naturally skeletonizes to reveal the many-holed cylindrical stems apparent in the descriptive botanical name. May be sprayed, altered, utilized as auxiliary stems for dried leaves in designs and for craft use, lamp stands, etc. Available from suppliers. The flat pads of Opuntia *platyocantha* may be skeletonized, resulting in a fan-shaped transparent form that can be dyed. Use as mass filler or interest area.

ORCHIDS Results vary with species. Some Vandas and Cypripidiums (Wild Moccasin Flower) are too delicate and tissuelike to handle successfully. Cattleyas, Cymbidiums, Oncidiums, Dendrobiums and Phalaenopsis deserve the most careful silica-gel handling (4 to 9 days). If you have access to a supply or want to experiment with your corsage (no need to disassemble it) the results may surprise you. I recently left a large purple and white Cattleya corsage lying on a dresser, and it air-dried with surprisingly little shrinkage or color loss, though the form should have been supported during the process. Air-dry the straplike leaves for linear work.

OSAGE ORANGE Deciduous native tree. Chartreuse inedible fruits may be semipreserved whole by alcohol-shellacking. May be sprayed vivid colors. The unusual bumpy texture adds character to interest areas. For use in contriveds, slice with sharp knife or electric saw, dry in 175-degree F. oven 24 hours. After about 12 hours, hook-wire. Oven-dried Osages are rock-hard, last indefinitely. May also be air-dried when cut into very thin slices; add stems. Target form.

PALMS Cycas, Date, Fishtail, Sago, Palmetto, Royal. Available from suppliers, roadsides, yards. Palm hearts, embryos are beautifully textured target and linear forms of good size. Embryos are partially expanded date-palm leaves. Many spathes, ribbons, etc., may be soaked in warm water to make pliable for reshaping. The beaded whips of date palm may be reshaped to various linear patterns. Calyxes of coconut can be made into "roses" for wreaths, topiary. Palmetto and coconut foliage are suitable for weaving, curling.

PALO VERDE  Yard, roadside tree native to Southwest. Interestingly curved and textured branches and trunk. Dry green for excellent linear patterns and free-style designing.

PAMPAS GRASS  Native roadside plant. Long, striking beige plumes. Cut when well developed but before the silky plume explodes, to avoid "molting." Air-dry either hanging or standing. Dip-dye or spray. Use in all contemporary designs, also Far Eastern and Mexican interpretives.

PANDANUS (Screwpine)  Shrub and pot plant. Many species. Use long, long-lasting leaves as they are, or hang-dry. Self-dry the large, round, roughly textured fruits. Dip in shellac-alcohol or glue to prevent dropping sections. Available from suppliers. Target form, or wire to ends of in-scale decorative wood for new-concept approaches.

PANSY, VIOLET, VIOLA  Biennial, perennial border plants. Violet foliage retains color, form, texture when treated 3 days in granular mix. Liquid-treated leaves go brownish in 10 days. Press flowers 3 to 4 days. Violets (*V. odorata*) are unsatisfactory pressed as the color "creams." Pansy and Viola press and take to granular treatment happily. All may need petal gluing. Even when carefully dried, pansies may draw moisture and "wilt" in humid weather. Store with crystals. Use in traditional tussy-mussies (those old-fashioned tight nosegays surrounded by paper frills that are again popular), spring and garden interpretives, and pictures. Small target.

DOGTOOTH VIOLETS: Not a violet but member of lily family. Native. Granular treatment 3 to 4 days;

press 6 to 7. Yellow hue holds beautifully.

PAPYRUS (Paper Reed)  Available from suppliers, greenhouse or warm-climate gardens. Stand to air-dry. Modern or Egyptian interpretive designs. Large-end linear form.

PASSION-FLOWER  Greenhouse or yard vine. Pink, red, purple, white. Refrigerate several days before pressing approximately 21 days, or granular-treat 2 to 10 days, checking progress often. Cover carefully to maintain unique form. Distinctive in modern, abstract and religious interpretive designs. Target form.

PEONY  White, pink, red, yellow hybrids. Singles, Japanese, and Anemone types dry faster than semi and fully double (bomb) types. Flower buds may be air-dried. (Also see dry storage under Semipermanent Processes, Chapter 7, as peonies respond to this holding method.) For granular drying, 2 to 8 days depending on type; test daily. Foliage granular-dried 3 to 5 days and taped to extender stems, or in liquid #2 for 2 weeks, but good results are sporadic. Peony seed pods are distinctive. Flowers are target, buds and pods are linear, and foliage is for mass-filler forms.

PEPPERS  Tropical shrub, home gardens. Air-dry (except Bell type) or dry slowly in 150-degree F. oven. Add natural extender stems or wire. Colors remain bright, shiny. Use in modern designs as linear or target forms. Bell or Sweet Peppers may be granular-dried. Cut fruit into four sections, leaving attached at stem end; remove seeds; dry several weeks. Use the rock-hard, dark green crinkle-textured forms in contriveds (which see), or mount on stem-extenders. Releasing target form.

PERIWINKLE (*Vinca minor,* Creeping Myrtle) Trailing plant. Wire small lavender or white flowers before granular-drying for 3 days. Use alone in small designs or bind on long wires for linear and cascading effects. Press flowers 5 to 8 days. Process delicate curving leafy stems in liquid #2 for 6 days, or lay in granular mix 7 to 8 days. May also be spray-painted any color while still fresh; cover both sides of the leaf, air-dry. Excellent in period mass designs (French, etc.) also in modern works, and for foliage in corsages, miniatures. *V. major* is larger, less hardy; has blue flowers. Treat same way.

PETUNIA Annual border plant. The delicate substance of petunias precludes much success; try granular-drying at your own risk. Small singles in many colors press in 5 days. Small target.

PHILODENDRON AND MONSTERA DELICIOSA Pot plants. Deeply lobed dark green, shiny target foliage. Treat in liquid #1. Monstera has large conical seed pods often available from suppliers.

PINE (Ponderosa, Alpine, Sugar, etc.) Evergreen native and yard trees. Long green needles in tufts on rough gray stems which are often interestingly curved. The tufts may be scissored to various shapes. Air-dry. Retains green color several months, then lightly spray with floral green. Or stand young fresh branches in liquid #1 for 10 days. Watch for gnarled twisted branches,

ideal in linear work. Use in Oriental-influenced, modern, abstract designs.

PINEAPPLE Perennial herb. Symbol of hospitality. Long-lasting addition to fruit and harvest portrayals. Rosettes of leaves granular-dry in 8 days, for releasing target form. *Ananas comosus,* a dwarf variety (3 inches in diameter), retains shape when air-dried whole.

POINCIANA, ROYAL Tropical tree, shrub. Long flat pods of interesting shape noteworthy in modern designs; may be split to take advantage of interior texture. Available from suppliers.

POINSETTIA Garden shrub and pot plant. Red, pink, white flowers formed by the petallike bracts. Excellent when pressed (7 days), but red dulls and needs spraying. Sear ends before processing. Target form. Granular-treated 5 days.

POMEGRANATE Tropical and greenhouse bush. Hard-rind, round, orange-red fruits. Air-dry slowly for 6 months. Drill a hole in stem end and mount on branches. Paint if you wish. Dry buds and the lovely rosette calyx by hanging upside down.

POPLAR (*Populus alba*) White or silver leaf. Deciduous native yard tree with white or grayish down on reverse leaf surface. Liquid #1 for 3 days. The white undersides are barely darkened while the upper surface becomes brownish black. May also be air-dried by cutting and hanging and later soaking 30 minutes in warm water before pressing under light weights. Time is thus saved in busy season by postponing pressing to a time when fewer plants demand attention. Effective when used as fine filler in mass and massed line designs.

PRIMROSE Evening Primrose is not *Primula* but *Cenothera biennis*. Granular-dry small brilliant yellow poppylike flowers 3 to 5 days. Excellent line when glued to branches of other plants; or add fine wire, hook method, for corsages. Press 6 days. Small target.

PRIMULA (Primrose) Perennial border herb. Common bright yellow low-growing primrose flowers (hook-wired) dry in silica gel 24 hours. Color holds beautifully for corsage work. The so-called Desert Primrose is a weeping dark-brown linear plant with short bristles forming brushlike ends. The Desert Birdcage or Lantern is a part of this plant. Air-dry. Unusual in mobiles, etc.

PROTEA Tropical shrub from florists or dried from suppliers. Proteas defy description because of lack of family resemblance; some look like daisies, artichokes, spider chrysanthemums, water-lilies. The large flower heads of scaly, highly colored bracts hold freshness 3 weeks when cut, and then dry hard, fading to soft tints of original hues, making them colorful additions—a popular and intriguing floral find.
BANKSIA, a member of the Protea family, is treated and used similarly. Flower and seed pod available from florists and suppliers. The handsome, long, narrow green foliage may be air-dried as it stands in the design.

PUFFBALLS See SALSIFY or ARTICHOKE or CARDOON.

PUSSY WILLOW Native and cultivated tree, shrub. Willowy branches closely covered with large silver or pinkish-gray catkins (aments). Collect when "pussies" are well formed. May be wired to curves when fresh. Air-dry. Lovely in many designs, especially spring interpretives. Wire tips for corsages.

PYRACANTHA Firethorn. Trailing yard shrub, various species. Dip into alcohol shellac for semipermanent red-berried linear forms. Alternate method is to place in 1 inch of water in dark place until moisture evaporates. Leaves drop, so remove them. Branches will also stay fresh for weeks if soaked under water overnight.

QUEEN-ANNE'S-LACE Parsley family. Roadside herb. Filmy white flowers in large umbels give many designs a fairylike look. Granular mix 5 to 7 days. Also collect delicate seed pods. Its cultivated cousin, Blue Lace, a big seller in florists' shops, may also be dried. Use in corsages, miniatures, as delicate mass filler.

RHODODENDRON See AZALEA.

ROOTS, TUBERS, RHIZOMES, BULBS, etc. Used in many ways in various abstract and avant-garde designs. Air-dry. Corn roots, well washed, used upside down, and mounted on stem extenders are startling examples.

ROSE Native and cultivated upright and vining shrub. Wide color range but yellows, oranges, whites, pinks accept drying most amiably. Select buds and half- to three-quarter-open blooms for best results. Full-blown roses are disappointing by any method, except when han-

DRIED FLOWERS WITH ELEGANCE  *The opulence of a bygone era is reflected in the formal dining room of the Governor's Palace in Colonial Williamsburg. Here a dignified massed design of artemesias, strawflowers, honesty, celosia, goldenrod, dock, pearly everlasting, and white poplar leaves honors a beautiful setting. Edna Pennell, designer for Colonial Williamsburg, Virginia.*

[*G. Rossner photo*]

dling single varieties such as Dainty Bess. Air-drying is easiest but results in considerable shrinkage, wrinkling and color alteration. Glue petals either before or after granular-drying. Leave 2 to 8 days depending on whether single or double forms. Check often. Dry cluster-type polyanthas and small floribundas (The Fairy) 3 to 4 days on fine wire stems or leave in the natural cluster, including the foliage. Miniature roses (dried 2 to 4 days) are unsurpassed in tiny designs, but the foliage is usually a bit oversized for a 5-inch miniature, in which no piece should

be more than ½ inch in diameter for perfect scale. Single and small varieties press beautifully in 7 days.

ROSE HIPS are semipermanent, usually red fruits. Dip in alcohol-shellac.

ROSE CANES are flexible, stay green for some time, and may be sprayed for modern and abstract work. Use some upside down so the prickles or thorns go the wrong way for weird effect. *Rosa omeiensis*, a shrub rose, has enormous deep-red thorns on wide-winged bases.

ROSE FOLIAGE: Hanging causes unattractive curling. Dry in granular mix 2 to 4 days for color retention. Treat in liquid #1 or in liquid #2 for 8 to 12 days for a warm brown color and flexibility. Heavy foliage (Peace) responds to liquid #2. Dried blooms can be reattached to original processed stems and leaves.

RUBBER-PLANT (*Ficus*) Pot or greenhouse plant. Heavy leaves may be skeletonized, liquid-treated, air-dried, pressed; or will serve as semi-permanent additions that hold up weeks in a design without water. Leaves laid on flat surface or hung will distort interestingly for strong modern and abstract elements. Success will be increased when using the liquid #1 method if a small portion of the main stalk is left with the leaf. Leaves without any stalk remnant should be submerged in liquid #2. Allow 10 to 12 days for either process. Boiling in soapy water whitens rubber-plant leaves.

SALAL (Lemon) Evergreen shrub. Florist standby often included with cut flowers Rather large heart-shaped leaves may be removed from branches, laid flat or placed in granular mix 4 days. Reassemble on heavier wire if a natural branch effect is desired or use individually in many types of design and wedding decorations. May be color-altered, drys naturally to soft green. Leaves can also be skeletonized to use with smaller-scaled flowers.

SANSEVIERIA (Snakeplant) Pot plant. Thick erect long leaves, green and variegated. Dry natural for linear form.

SALSIFY (Goatsbeard or Puffball) Roadside plant. Color-spray or plastic-fix round gossamer puffs as they stand by the roadside. Gather a few while there are still green buds and stand in a bottle to open at will. They will puff to a smaller size for gradations to delight the designer. Terrific additions to mobiles, moderns, avant-garde designs, contriveds.

SALVIA (Sage) Border herbs, shrubs. Spikes, racemes, and panicles on tall stems. Best known and most used is Scarlet Sage (*S. splendens*). It may be hang-dried; though the flower petals drop, the bracts retain color. The spikes dried for 4 days in granular mix turn Chinese red. Treat Blue Salvia (*S. farinacea*) in the fall for deeper color when air-dried. Both types press nicely in 5 to 7 days.

SCOTCH BROOM Roadside in South and Northwest. Available from pod catalogs. The long stringlike, nearly leafless stems are valued by arrangers for establishing linear patterns. Dry naturally, in which case they remain green but become brittle. Liquid #1 keeps them pliable but darkens the color to near black. May be sprayed, dyed, sparkled. May be soaked and reshaped after drying. The yellow pealike flowers may be pressed 7 to 10 days. Dried Scotch broom will last several years without deterioration.

SILVER-LACE (Fleece-Vine) Spray with plastic to set before drying and prevent petal drop. Treat with granular mix 3 to 4 days. The graceful tendrils are fine for mass or cascade designs and linear curves.

SKUNK CABBAGE Native swamp plant sometimes called Swamp-Ginger. Clear bright yellow spadix and spathe. Natural-dry by standing on a pinholder 10 to 12 days, but expect shrinkage. Dry in granular mix 3 to 5 days. Spray spathe vivid orange or green for unusual impact. The exotic form is a find for newer-concept work. Process large bright green foliage 3 to 7 days in granular mix.

SNAPDRAGON Border plant. Pink and yellow pastels and white are the most satisfactory. Dry wired florets separately in granular mix 3 to 4 days. The top 3 to 4 inches of the main spike, which carries the buds and partially opened flowers, may be laid flat in the mix and dried 5 to 7 days. Reassemble spike. The flower spike with all florets intact dries well in 8 days, but shrinking widens spaces between florets; also florets are easily knocked off in handling. Flowers press well; allow 7 to 10 days. Use spikes as linear forms in many designs; individual florets in corsages, miniatures.

SOY BEAN Annual herb. When bleached, the twisted flattened stems and contorted round cluster of pods are exciting additions to modern and abstract designing. Available from pod shops.

SPIREA Deciduous shrub. Pinkish red or white flowers in arching sprays (Bridal Wreath, *S. vanhouttei*), in spikes (*S. billiardi*) and flattish clusters (*S. Anthony Waterer*). All dry well in granular mix 4 to 7 days. Use small clusters in miniature and small designs, others in linear and target areas. Leave foliage on Bridal Wreath. Fine filler, linear, and interest-area plants.

SQUASH Garden vegetable. Scrape out the meat, bake shell until hard at 200 degrees F. Shellac or oil for use as container or accessory, depending upon shape. Or cut to resemble flower petals before drying. See Contrived What-Is-Its, Chapter 6. Air-dry large lobed leaves by laying between several newspapers, unweighted. Dampen slightly after drying to regain three-dimensional form.

STRAWFLOWER Border annual. Many colors. Cut in bud to one-half open; if cut later flowers will continue to mature and pop their centers. Hook-wire. Long-lasting. Excellent in small designs and grouped in massed-line, mass designs; use in corsages, contriveds, and summer wreaths.

STRELITZIA (Bird-of-Paradise) Tropical herb. Border plant in warm climates; pot plant, greenhouse plant or from florist in most areas. Hang the long leaves upside down for fascinating forms. The showy blossoms, borne in rigid boatlike bracts, have several petals united to form a "tongue"; these shrink when air-dried. The bracts may be used in contrived forms and large-end linear work. Strelitzia are available from pod shops dyed to look natural. Leaves and blooms are spectacular in avant-garde, newer-concept and Egyptian interpretive designs.

SUMAC Tree or shrub, native and cultivated. Dense torches of crimson fruitlike seed heads, which are velvety in the fall, may also be gathered when young and green (stand to dry). Air-dry for long-lasting linear or target forms. Pick the foliage at fall's color peak, package-press 4 to 5 days. Gather twisted branches of strong linear pattern and glue clusters of bright red leaves treated in granular mix 4 to 6 days to the tips; use as free-form shapes in free-style designs.

SUNFLOWER   Native and border annual and perennial herb. Sizes vary from small to colossal. Granular-treat flowers 3 to 10 days, depending on size. To press the immense ones, remove the petals, dry individually in granular mix, and then reglue onto the air-dried center disks. For mod effects, spray the disk white and the petals black before reassembling. Press small-flowered varieties 7 to 10 days. Sunflower "trumpets" can be made by removing all seeds when the head is freshly picked; remove center by running a sharp knife around outer edges. It will peel away easily. Hang-dry the empty cup in a warm dark place and spray vivid colors for dramatic target forms in newer-concept designs. May be soaked and reshaped. Foliage can be skeletonized, pressed or granular-treated. Use as mass filler or target forms.

WESTERN PRAIRIE SUNFLOWER is *Balsamorhiza*, called Balsam-Root. Treat same as sunflower.

SWEET GUM (*Liquidambar styraciflua*)   Deciduous tree. All parts are eminently usable in many types of floral work. The shining maplelike leaves turn brilliant scarlet in early fall (cut before frost to retain color) and may be treated with liquid #1 to retain red hues permanently. The foliage may also be pressed 4 to 5 days. When bare of leaves, the erect corky winged branches with deeply fissured bark serve as strong structural lines. The dark brown persistent spiny fruit balls gathered in late fall are exceedingly ornamental in wreaths, topiaries, corsages, and contrived forms.

SWEET PEA   Annual or perennial vining plant. Process florets individually 2 to 4 days in granular mix, reassemble. Use in mass, massed-line, and small designs.

TANSY   Similar to Yarrow though of different family. See YARROW.

TEASEL   Coarse thistlelike roadside perennial, also available from florists and pod suppliers. Dense heads with embracing bracts which are sharp and spiny. Harvest when dry (dark brown) on their strong natural (but prickly) stems. Also may be picked when small and green. Air-dry. Useful as parts for contrived flower forms (Chapter 7), and as linear forms in many types of design. Very decorative when used in wreaths, novelties, topiary trees, etc.

THISTLE   Roadside and border high.

GLOBE THISTLE (*Echinops*) has metallic-blue flower-studded balls on long sturdy stems. Gather before the tiny flowers open and dry upside down for 12 days. When picked in the green immature stage, the balls dry very well to soft avocado gray. Handle carefully; if picked when a bit over-mature, they shatter unmercifully. Spraying with glue, varnish, or plastic fixative may prevent this. Package-dry the bold prickly (white reverse) foliage which turns a clear crisp gray when air-dried. The globes are excellent line or vertical forms if remounted to twisty stems.

CANADIAN THISTLE, stalwart invader of Western pasture lands, has one redeeming feature in its lovely purple heads, which may be granular-dried 4 to 9 days. The stalks sometimes fasciate or are chemically contorted and are considered dramatic finds, but protect yourself with heavy gloves as the spines are vicious.

TI (*Cordyline*) Available from florists and grown as pot or greenhouse subjects. Beautiful broad leaves, all green or with various rosy hues and multi-red-yellows. Even after weeks in a fresh design, the leaves will dry soft brown if laid flat or hung. The form can be altered by gently manipulating the leaf spine while fresh, or, if dry, may be steamed to make pliable. Make some loops and folded forms, dry in that position for elegant variations. If leaves are fresh, stand in liquid #1 for 8 days. Leaves are broad enough to be cut out for abstract shapes and are excellent bold releasing target forms.

TULIPS Bulbous spring border flower. Pastels dry best. Cut before fully open, remove natural fleshy stem, hook-wire. Dry in granular mix 3 to 6 days. If flare is too prominent when removed from medium, add a dab of creamy or clear glue where the petals overlap, and hang upside down until dry. Excellent in mass, linear, modern, and spring-interpretive work. Dry a few fully opened blooms to obtain a large round form for focal areas. Collect the interesting seed pods when ripe. Heavy-textured tulip foliage may be liquid-treated, frozen and hung, or oven-dehydrated. Flowers respond to dry storage (which see).

UNICORN PLANT Martynia family, also called Devil's-Claw, Proboscis Flower. Annual, perennial border herb. Unique beaked seed pod which, when dried, looks like a fantastic bird or some prehistoric insect, depending on how it is turned. When dry, cut with a piece of the parent stem attached, drill small holes, insert pipe-cleaner legs. The "birds" can be sprayed or dabbed with a "face." Beads, felt, etc., may be added in many amusing ways. The "claws," which nature made to aid the seeds' hitchhiking on animal fur, make interesting additions to holiday novelties such as wreaths, topiary work. When mounted on own stems or those of other plants, the pod takes on a surrealistic form appropriate for contemporary work.

VIBURNUM Deciduous and evergreen yard shrub. The handsome foliage of many species can be treated either with liquid #1 or #2; experiment with the variety available to you. Some species have long-lasting red or blue-black bloomy fruits which benefit from the shellac-alcohol treatment. The flower clusters or balls (as in the common Snowball, *V. opulus sterile*) can be granular-treated 5 to 9 days with varying results. *V. carlesia* (pink, white) does excellently in silica gel for 5 days. Remove stems and wire after drying to auxiliary stems. Use small clusters in miniatures. Leatherleaf, *V. rhytidophyllum*, is an excellent subject.

VINCA MINOR, MAJOR See PERIWINKLE.

VIOLET See PANSY.

WATER-HEMLOCK (Wild-Parsley)

Native perennial marsh herb. Small white flowers in flat, rounded umbels. Harvest when dry; no further treatment is needed. The large starry seed head is unsurpassed for modern and abstract effects. Spray, sparkle, flock, crystallize. Gather on the long natural stems. Stems need no further support and are hollow, so they serve well as extenders for dried leaves and large flowers of other plants. Clusters last for years, and if a starlet is knocked off, merely glue it back. The clusters lend themselves to all kinds of contrived constructions as well as serving as interest points in mobiles, stamobiles, contemporary designs.

POISON HEMLOCK is a coarse roadside herb which is treated and used the same way. Both plants are poisonous, particularly the roots of the latter, which are said to have been used to make the death drink of the Greek philosopher Socrates. But neither is dangerous unless eaten.

WILD-PARSLEY See WATER-HEMLOCK.

WILLOW Erect and weeping native and cultivated tree, shrub. Also see PUSSY-WILLOW. Long flexible branches valuable for linear work. Wire or peg fresh branches in curves, which air-dry permanently. Or fasten to coat hanger pulled to desired shape and bake in slow oven (200 degrees F.) 1 hour for rich brown color. Willow is also often used in making kubari (holders) for Oriental designing. Kilmarnock Willow (*Salix pendula*) has crooked branches excellent for linear effects, and one variety of *Salix chermesina* has brilliant red twigs. Corkscrew Willow (*Salix matsudana tortuosa*) or Fantail Willow gives contorted branches, great for Oriental and eerily twisted mod free-style designs. May be peeled.

WOODBINE (Virginia-Creeper) Garden and woods vine. Large five-lobed leaves turn red in the fall. Process either green or red in granular mix 10 to 12 days or package-process 2 to 3 weeks. Useful as mass filler and cascade.

WOOD ROSES Seed pods of the Hawaiian morning glory available from florists, pod shops. Hard woody pods resemble brown roses. Use as small target forms in designs and include in contriveds, wreaths, corsages.

YARROW (*Achillea millefolium*) and TANSY (*Tanacetum vulgare*) Herbaceous roadside and border perennials. White, pink, yellow flower heads (Tansy has only yellow). Cut all species soon as mature. Air-drying is satisfactory, though granular mix for 4 to 5 days gives brighter color. Yarrow's lacy foliage also dries well; simply lay on flat surface. Use as target forms in contemporary designs with foliage as filler.

YUCCA Herbaceous and treelike roadside plants. Many species. Stiff swordlike leaves often have broad yellow bases. Air-dry or process in liquid #1. Granular-treat creamy white blossom spires 10 days. Collect seed pods before frost, air-dry either in clusters on the natural stem or individually wired or glued to other stems to meet many design needs.

Bleach or spray. Excellent in contrived work.

ZINNIA Border herb. Sear ends. Press singles 5 days, doubles 7 days. In granular treatment, if the natural stem is retained, dry 4 to 6 days, less if wire stems are substituted. Curled-petal types and singles dry best. Use as target forms in traditional mass, massed-line and modern arrangements.

# ❧❧❧ INDEX

# About the Author

Esther Veramae Hamél—author of *The Encyclopedia of Judging & Exhibiting*, former editor of *Montana Gardens*, lecturer and flower show judge from Canada to California, and civic leader—has received wide recognition from the National Council of State Garden Clubs, Inc., and from horticultural organizations in her own state of Montana. She has served fourteen years as a director of National Council, is an instructor in Flower Arrangement and Flower Show Practice, a Master Judge, and National Chairman of the Landscape Critics Council. Her honors include: the Council's Presidential Award in 1968, the Montana Federation of Garden Clubs' Cup for Advancing Gardening in Montana in 1957, Montana Gardener of the Year in 1958, with a Special Achievement Award in 1969. Mrs. Hamél is included in *Who's Who Among Western Women*, *Who's Who Among American Women*, *The Dictionary of International Biography*, and *The Directory of British and American Writers*. The author lives on a ranch in Montana with her husband, who is a supervisor in the Agricultural Stabilization and Conservation Service, is the mother of a son and daughter, and has two grandchildren.